SpringerBriefs in Political Science

More information about this series at http://www.springer.com/series/8871

Anja Mihr

Cyber Justice

Human Rights and Good Governance for the Internet

Springer

Anja Mihr
Center on Governance through Human Rights
HUMBOLDT-VIADRINA Governance Platform
Berlin, Germany

ISSN 2191-5466 ISSN 2191-5474 (electronic)
SpringerBriefs in Political Science
ISBN 978-3-319-60091-8 ISBN 978-3-319-60093-2 (eBook)
DOI 10.1007/978-3-319-60093-2

Library of Congress Control Number: 2017942799

Printed on acid-free paper

This Springer imprint is published by Springer Nature
The registered company is Springer International Publishing AG
The registered company address is: Gewerbestrasse 11, 6330 Cham, Switzerland

Contents

List of Abbreviations

ACTA	Anti-Counterfeiting Trade Agreement
ARF	ASEAN Regional Forum
AU	African Union
CAC	Cyberspace Administration of China
CoE	Council of Europe
CSO	Civil Society Organization
CSR	Corporate Social Responsibility
ECJ	European Court for Justice
ECtHR	European Court of Human Rights
EFF	Electronic Frontier Foundation
EU	European Union
HRD	Human rights defenders
IANA	International Assigned Numbers Authority
ICANN	Internet Corporation for Assigned Names and Numbers
ICC	International Criminal Court
ICCPR	UN International Convention on Civil and Political Rights
ICESCR	International Covenant on Economic, Social and Cultural Rights
ICJ	International Court of Justice
IGF	Internet Governance Forum
IP	Internet Protocols
ITU	International Telecommunication Union
MAG	Multistakeholder Advisory Group
NSA	National Security Agency
OAS	Organization for American States
OSCE	Organization for Security and Cooperation in Europe
PIPA	IP Protection Act Preventing Real Online Threats to Economic Creativity and Theft of Intellectual Property Act
PPP	Public–Private Partnerships
SCO	Shanghai Cooperation Organization
SDGs	Sustainable Development Goals

SOPA	Stop Online Privacy Act
UDHR	Universal Declaration for Human Rights
UN	United Nations
WSIS	World Summit on the Information Society

Chapter 1
Introduction

Cyber justice is a viable approach for defining how good governance and human rights norms can be guiding principles to govern the Internet. Cyberspace is a borderless public space in which the Internet is a network and a tool that allows different digital devices to connect and communicate. Cyberspace has more and more been converted into "one space" in which we move at the same time in an online and an offline space. But the main difference between the offline and online space and the world we live and work in is that the online space lacks justifiability and liability of actors and institutions that provide online services that we use.

Whereas there is no longer a controversy whether international human rights norms and standards are valid norms, offline as well as online, the controversy is around the way, the means, and the litigability of these norms and standards being used in the Internet and the services it provides, i.e., social media, online banking, data storage, and transfer. The question around cyber justice is, thus, *who* should be held accountable and *how* in a borderless "space" that does not pose yet any democratic governance regime as we know it from territorial and statehood-based countries?

Thus far, cyberspace is a space without common and globally agreed enforceable rules or governance bodies because it lacks legislative or judiciary bodies equally accessible for all, such as a cyber court and a government, a bureaucracy, a police, or a parliament that would manage people's activities within that space globally and protect users' rights and entitlements.

Worldwide, these challenges are well acknowledged and various international and national governmental and nongovernmental approaches aim to develop a form of "Internet governance" or "cyber governance." The United Nations (UN), for example, along with other regional international organizations, such as the Council of Europe (CoE), the European Union (EU), the Organization for American States (OAS), the NATO, the G7 and G20, the Shanghai Cooperation Organization (SCO), the ASEAN Regional Forum (ARF), the BRICS, or the African Union (AU), have undertaken various efforts to use international and domestic governmental tools to regulate the cyberspace. However, they face challenges as they

A. Mihr, *Cyber Justice*, SpringerBriefs in Political Science,
DOI 10.1007/978-3-319-60093-2_1

realize that one state or a group of governments alone cannot regulate nor protect sufficiently our privacy and rights in cyberspace. Cyber justice is thus still far from being achieved.

Albeit court decisions by the Inter-American Court of Human Rights, the European Court of Justice (ECJ) or the European Court of Human Rights (ECtHR) has established case law over the past years that could lead to a future global judiciary for all four billion "cyber citizens." Yet, international court decisions are far from being fully implemented, because there is not one state or one particular actor located in one specific country that can protect data and safeguard our human rights alone. Charging Google Europe for deleting personal information about one specific person from its search profile will still allow Internet users in other parts of the world to access the same information and data of that person outside of Europe. The claim for the "right to be forgetten" soon became the "right to have one's privacy protected," but it cannot fully be safeguarded without full accordance of rules and regulations at the global level. The judgments and decisions on whether to keep our data private do not have any specific addressee; governments as well as private companies are responsible for safeguarding our privacy. Sometimes, it is governmental institutions, such as security agencies, and sometimes private companies or social media channels, such as YouTube or WhatsApp, which sell and disseminate our data without our prior consent. Generally speaking, the limits of "free floating data" and the harm it can do to people's personal lives and their developments are not fully investigated yet. Defining violence in cyberspace by the intransparency of data flow and of making private data public without the fully informed consent by the owner—usually us users—of the data is a violation of human rights in many aspects: the human right to privacy, to information, to movement, to development, to security and safety, and even to physical integrity in case of widespread hate speech and cyber mobbing.

The current "Wild West" situation in cyberspace might remind us how European colonizers in the eighteenth century asked illiterate natives of the respective territory to sign contracts and agreements they could neither read nor understand while keeping them in the belief that these "papers" would guarantee their full independence and rights as promised. The opposite became true. Their "promised lands" were stolen, their cultures and identities largely destroyed, and their future generations were often deprived of full integration and developments. Inequality and violent outbreaks are the consequence of these practiced until today. The comparison to colonizers' practices and today's practices of private and governmental service providers in the Internet might be far-fetched and yet similarities are present. For example, when we quickly press the consent button on cookies or Amazon and Instagram privacy policies in full trust that Facebook and others keep their promise that our data is only used for the companies' commercial interest or it is accessible only to our online "friends," here, we still do not fully understand or control what happens to our data and who uses or misuses it. Instead of sharing our bank details, health data with our health insurance, and private pictures with Instagram, many of us might instead "consent" that their freedoms, self-determination, and privacy are jeopardized.

How to govern or regulate this space, and its providers and users, has had many attempts over the past decades aiming to lead to a new global governance regime based on human rights norms, good governance, and multistakeholder principles. The Internet Governance Forum (IGF) under the UN is one of many global efforts to define the future governance regime. It is needed more than ever, since the large distribution of mobile device and Internet protocol (IP) addresses in the Global South has also contributed to more mobility among people. Today's mass migrations, forced or deliberately, would not be possible without the Internet and the information, orientation, and communication services it provides. IPv6, for example, is an association that sells and provides new IP addresses particularly in the Global South, knowing that the next generation of cyber citizens is standing in line (World IPV6 Launch 2016). The difference between the previous generation of IP distribution of IPv4 addresses and the new generation of IP addresses is that IPv6 is more traceable and no longer anonymous. Thus, in the future, individual users and people who provide services or post data on the Internet will be easier to identify and held accountable for wrongdoings in cyberspace and misuse of data than in present times. But World IP is a private enterprise and a global neutral control mechanism which is issuing these addresses and controlling them is currently not possible, although the UN IGF has undertaken some efforts in 2016 to establish such independent monitoring bodies. The fact that new IP addresses are mostly distributed in Global South countries, where there is little to no rule of law, a lack of independent judiciary, and often a poor record of human rights, allows for the assumption that Internet users in the Global South are mostly out of independent control. Opposition and political activists in these countries can easily be caught and stopped for their opposition movements by the governments. And service providers or hackers who misuse private data for commercial or criminal interests can do so without fearing much of governmental or international control and repercussions.

In 2016, the CoE launched the net neutrality guidelines of compulsory indications for its 47 member states ranging from Portugal to Russia and from Turkey to Iceland. Although this guideline has only regional impact, it clearly defines the responsibilities in the struggle for who is responsible to provide best and neutral access to cyberspace, which are governments, not private corporates such as Google or Amazon. It states that "national authorities should monitor and issue public reports on Internet traffic management practices" and that Internet traffic should be treated equally, without discrimination, restriction, or interference irrespective of the sender, receiver, content, application, service, or device (Directorate of Communication 2016).

The importance of net neutrality in current developments is illustrated by a study of the University of Konstanz in Germany and the Swiss Federal Institute of Technology, ETH, in Zürich. Researchers looked at 118 countries and addressed around 500 different ethnic, indigenous, and marginalized communities who were excluded and discriminated because of their remote location, their income, or their social status to have free and neutral access to the Internet. At the same time, the main resource to mobilize their communities to participate in public policies of their countries in order to change their situation is the Internet. But even if their leaders and spokespersons have access to the Internet, their constituency does not necessarily have it. Thus, these users are often excluded from the promise that the Internet seems to give, namely, a tool to free and emancipate those who have been far too long marginalized because of their ethnicity, gender, income, or other criteria (BETA 2016, p. 905).

As early as 1988, the first debates about the level of accountability and neutrality of services and providers in the Internet were discussed. At that time, less than 1% of the world's population even understood the term "Internet." In an article by David Clark on the anticipated future role of IP addresses to protect users' rights and entitlements, he quotes the debates among governments at that time, namely, that the "resource used in the Internet architectures must be an accountable one" to their stakeholders, that is to say, whoever uses or provides information or data, services, or networks on the Internet and in cyberspace must be held accountable for her or his postings (Clark 1988, p. 107). At the early times of the Internet in the 1980s, this debate took place among national intelligence agencies, hardware developers, and software programmers, all highlighting the fact that the Internet would in the future not only provide useful services for civilians and the military alike, but that this would pose a serious challenge for the security and safety of the flow of information and data in cyberspace. The anticipated problems of 1988 became a reality in the time period of 2013 when whistleblowers such as Edward Snowden leaked military and other intelligence information to the wider public. The importance of the new technologies for national defense, thus involving the military and security sector, was already anticipated long before its civil use, which commenced 10 years later. But among others, one of the main problems at that time was seen in the "management" of the Internet, which we call Internet or cyber governance today. As Clark phrased it almost 30 years ago, "the most important change in the Internet architecture over the next few years will probably be the development of a new generation of tools for the management of resources in the context of multiple administrations" of the Internet (Clark 1988, p. 113).

There is no lack of international human rights norms and standards, as defined by the UN and other regional human rights regimes and their definitions of freedom rights and privacy. Human rights have also entered the world of cyber conferences over the past years despite its usual strong technological focus. The same has been true for good governance norms and rules, such as the question about accountability, transparency, and interaction among those who use the Internet and those who manage and provide Internet services. One of the major challenges in this area is how to establish, increase, or leverage public "user" trust in the Internet and its various service providing agencies. Internet users' behavior adapts to the pitfalls and challenges of the Internet and its lawless and noncontrollable space, but yet it penetrates the private domains of millions of people. Once the confidence and trust in certain Internet tools is lost, it is difficult to restore it. Instead, Internet users often react with self-censorship or by not using services. This could have an impact on their personal development and well-being such as our health and access to education. The same accounts for human rights defenders (HRD), such as lawyers, teachers, social workers, judges, CSOs, and so on, whose activities on the Internet are sometimes the only form of protest against offline and online human rights violation and suppression. But their space of action and interventions is shrinking by the possibilities security agencies and governments have in tracing HRD back via their use of Internet platforms (Mihr 2016). At the same time, HRD and online activists self-censor and shrink their own spaces by not using certain tools due to the fear of being reported to security agencies and police or being tracked down and then suffering physical offline consequences.

Clark's vision of 1988 all became true and more complex than he had anticipated more than a generation ago. It has been a long way from the idea of accountability, management, and an effective governance regime that upholds cyber justice. Cyber justice, thus, ought to be based on good governance through a human rights-based approach to safeguard freedom and privacy rights as well as those of human development and security. At the same time, it ought to increase the accountability of the rights and duty bearers; the transparency of providers and users; and more participation and interaction among states, nonstates, private users, and providers to agree on common norms, on rules, and on independent mechanisms on how to uphold them. Being able to hold everyone accountable, regardless of whether state agency or private ones, is the aim of cyber justice.

This booklet will give a brief overview of some of the achievements toward the concept of cyber justice over the past two decades as well as current and future endeavors that go beyond cybersecurity or cyber governance but also deal with ethical and philosophical questions raised in the context of human rights, law, governance, and social contract.

References

BETA. (2016). *Wir fordern digitale Grundrechte: Charta der digitalen Grundrechte der Europäischen Union.*. Accessed December 1, 2016, from http://www.digitalcharta.eu

Clark, D. D. (1988). The design philosophy of the DARPA internet protocols. *Computer Communication Review, 18*(4), 106–114.

Directorate of Communication. (2016). *Council of Europe issues network neutrality guidlines to protect freedom of expression and privacy*. Press Release – DC003 (2016). Council of Europe. Accessed January 1, 2017, from https://wcd.coe.int/ViewDoc.jsp?p=&id=2402819&direct=true

Mihr, A. (2016). Cyber justice: Cyber-governance through human rights and a rule of law in the internet. *US-China Law Review, 13*(4), 314–336.

World IPV6 Launch. (2016). *IPV6 is the new normal.*. Accessed December 1, 2016, from http://www.worldipv6launch.org/

Chapter 2
Cyber World

Good cyber governance fosters human rights and protects them through technologies that operate in a global borderless public space in which individuals, regardless of their citizenship, nationality, ethnicity, political orientation, or gender, communicate and interact. These individual users of cyberspace and the Internet conduct businesses, make politics, and organize their private lives in this space. The Internet itself is a communication and management tool that is used for various private and societal purposes. It allows governments to inform citizens and to participate in public policies, for businesses to make transactions, for refugees to organize their pathways through the continents, for academics to exchange quicker and timely scientific results, for human rights organizations to inform and educate their supporters, for HRD to organize events, for civil society organizations to reach visibility, for friends to stay in contact, as far as for terror groups to mobilize their constituency for action. Millions of apps, social media, and research tools allow for access to education, health, news, financial markets, business, or contacts that otherwise would not be possible through snail mail, phone, fax, and other classical communication tools.

The term cyber has undergone a dramatic shift and expansion over the past two decades. Some criticize that the term has become too arbitrary and user-defined. Instead, as Wagner and Vieth claim, the term had its origin in the military and intelligence sector in the USA way back in the 1980s, as also illustrated earlier by the debate between Clark and the national security agencies in the USA. The origin of the term cyber in the military and security defense sector is one reason why today's terms and notions related to cyber often signal "threats" and "fears," such as cyber war, cyber viruses, or cyber terror. They are linked to cyberspace but not to civil and peaceful Internet tools as such. "Cyberization" of everything beyond the original purpose, according to Wagner and Vieth, is thus not responding to the needs and concerns of Internet users today. Instead of making best use of this space and see it as another sphere in which we operate our daily business and private lives, users see it sometimes as an ungoverned, immaterial, dubious, and violent space that creates more insecurity and fear than actually is the case (Wagner and Vieth 2016).

A. Mihr, *Cyber Justice*, SpringerBriefs in Political Science,
DOI 10.1007/978-3-319-60093-2_2

But today's cyber world does not adhere to any code of conduct (yet) or a cyber-constitution that would discipline or rule us, users and providers, and prevent us from the misuse and abuse of this communication and information tool through incentives or rules, laws, and repercussions. At the same time, people have rapidly adapted (often through self-censorship) to the challenges and threats that the possible breach of their data provides, in particular when it comes to their human right to privacy. These cyber-citizens or users have become more conscious of posting information and data that might potentially be used against them in international or national lawsuits—if those persons happen to physically touch ground in the respective country or territory. Consequently, it is possible to manage the behavior and to establish a rule of law for cyberspace. The two main avenues to pursue this are:

1. To establish a societal and legally binding "cyber constitution" as a type of "social contract"
2. To establish global enforcement and monitoring bodies, such as courts, multi-stakeholder committees, or otherwise rotating, participatory, and transparent governance regimes

As for the time being, the cyberspace and Internet do not have any enforceable common rules or standards, such as a government or governmental control. There are no globally agreed and adhered mechanisms that would protect and foster people's activities in this space, except for universal human rights norms. Universal human rights norms and standards or customary international law can serve as guidance and benchmarks for setting up governance regimes in cyberspace (United Nations Human Rights Office of the High Commissioner 2017). Through new technologies, cyberspace offers an environment that consists of many participants who have the ability to affect and influence each other. This space is transparent and neutral in its nature but often defined, broadened, limited, or censored by the people who use it. Communication via the Internet is therefore often anonymous and used and shared with the worldwide public, which remains, in large part, unknown to the individual Internet user, namely, each of us.

We, nonetheless, continue to share our most private and personal data with this anonymous audience. Today, there are around four billion Internet users. It is about half of the world's population. The majority is below 30 years of age and often has little or no experience with good governance principles but an urge for personal development, settlement of private life, and professional progress. If cyberspace would be a country, it would be the largest and most populated one in the world, albeit one without any constitution or government. It has no police or law enforcement mechanisms, let alone protection mechanisms for all Internet citizens to safeguard their rights and entitlements. This "country" has no legislative or otherwise democratic decision-making bodies. And why should we entrust our most private data to people or companies that privately claim to govern this territory? The answer would be because we have no other remedies to use the Internet and that we are in an urge to establish transparent and accountable governing bodies to regulate and rule the cyber world. Thus, time is running to create cyber justice regimes.

The two internationally defined human rights that are most in focus when considering cyberspace are that of freedom (or access to information and data) and privacy, that is to say the protection of our data. They are also often called "digital rights." But any benchmark on how and where to define freedom and privacy when using the Internet is yet missing. The Fundamental Rights Charta of the EU Lisbon Treaty from December 2009 defines the right to privacy as a sphere in which we enjoy and pursue our family life, friends, health, and personal development. In article 7 and 8 of the annexed Charta to the treaty, these rights are far reaching and not surprisingly encompass all aspects of life, including professional, private, and public development and progress if it is related to our personal and individual development. Claims for privacy aim to protect persons that run for public office in the same way as for someone who gets management training through an online education course and does not want his employer to know. Which of these data footprints that we leave behind when moving in the one world of cyberspace are meant to be made invisible for public eyes and which ones not and if so, who penalizes the data and by what criteria? Governments aim to regulate and ask network providers such as Facebook or Amazon to protect customers' data and if not propose penalties or compensations to the persons whose rights are violated. But thus far, no CEO of a service provider who leaked or sold data for commercial purposes or other reasons was ever penalized. Instead, whistleblowers have been penalized.

References

United Nations Human Rights Office of the High Commissioner. (2017). *Universal human rights index database*. Accessed April 1, 2017, from http://www.ohchr.org/EN/HRBodies/Pages/UniversalHumanRightsIndexDatabase.aspx

Wagner, B., & Vieth, K. (2016). Was macht Cyber? Epistemologie und Funktionslogik von Cyber. *Zeitschrift für Außen- und Sicherheitspolitik*, *9*(2), 213–222. Accessed April 1, 2017, from http://link.springer.com/article/10.1007/s12399-016-0557-1

Chapter 3
Human Rights

The only "rule" that exists to set limits to freedom and privacy human rights in cyberspace thus far is the "do no harm rule" derived from the maxim that many lawyers, judges, and advocates of human rights use to consider the possible harm that any intervention of freedom of expression, thoughts, or other actions might impact on others. This maxim serves many judges in particular at international courts, such as the ECtHR and tribunals, as a benchmark. It helps to distinguish nonviolent from violent and harmful actions. In the (almost) anarchical world of cyberspace, that rule aims to measure and evaluate when privacy or freedoms are at stake, for example, when freedom of expression becomes hate speech, or when posting private wedding pictures on Facebook for "friends only" and they shortly afterwards can be watched on the World Wide Web by everyone.

Generally speaking, neither our freedoms nor our privacy is violated if actions on the Internet do not lead or call to any physical harm of the integrity of a person or a group. Nevertheless, the way we interpret or understand the freedom of expression, information, or privacy will change in the future if more cases of people suffer harm because of postings in social media that eventually might lead to death and loss of work.

The worldwide media freedom and development index illustrates at a glance the correlation between freedom of media in the Internet (DW Akademie 2015). In regions with recent rapid growth in Internet access, namely, Africa and Asia, the freedom of media is dramatically low and the space in which freedom of expression, assembly, and information can be exchanged by users and providers shrink dramatically due to governmental interventions and self-censorship.

Thus far, Art 19 of the UN International Convention on Civil and Politica Rights (ICCPR) on freedom of expression is benchmarked against its limits such as hate speech if the latter threatens "public order" or the "rights of others," their equality, or right to nondiscrimination. If that is the case, the freedom can be limited. However, the fact that "public order" is interpreted differently in almost all countries and courts in the world does not make it easier to balance freedom against

A. Mihr, *Cyber Justice*, SpringerBriefs in Political Science,
DOI 10.1007/978-3-319-60093-2_3

security in the day-to-day cyber debate. The threshold of when a free opinion turns into harm of others depends on the severity of its intent, content, public extent, imminence, likelihood of probable action, and context in which it is expressed (Article 19, Global Campaign for Free Expression 2010). In some contexts, an expression can be funny and harmless. In a different context, the same expression can turn to hate crime and massive bodily harm of others.

That does not mean wikileakers or whistleblowers, let alone Facebook or Weibo, will be considered harmful per se if they disclose "confidential" material or hate speech to the public. The opposite is true if they contribute to the notion of neutral Internet. The tools and means the Internet provides in cyberspace often allows to shed light on the inside of institutions, organizations, or policy makers, lives that otherwise would have never been possible. This will continue to exist—with or without anticipated reactions. But the way we morally judge these disclosures, postings, and announcements will change. We will become more sensitive to these postings because we have learned the negative consequence that images or "funny" postings can have on us and others."Internet literacy," as some call it, aims for us to learn when postings, pictures, images, news, and films have harmful or otherwise jeopardizing consequences. An intentionally "harmless" or "funny" posting can have harmful consequences on individuals or institutions, including people who commit suicide because of wrongful or shameful postings on social media. The guiding principles to become "literate" is to distinguish harm from nonharm that Internet postings can lead to and define harm with every new cyber generation.

Some of the infringed and endangered human rights in cyberspace or freedom and individual political rights are that of expression, information, property, association, discrimination, and participation. But even the human rights to individual development and progress, women and children, and minority rights are under threat, because marginalized groups become more marginalized through acts of discrimination, geoblocking, or hate speech. The structure of the Internet, its pervasiveness, and the possibility it affords for anonymity have made cyberspace a playground for those who are full of anger, prejudice, and hatred and wish to spread harmful propaganda and incite hate and violence. A quick check on any search engine provided numerous home pages that target propaganda against immigrants, Jews, Muslims, women, and homosexuals. Those websites incite hate and encourage violence against these groups. International networks against cyber hate often receive public and state support to notify, make transparent, and alarm policy makers to interfere in these actions (Zarrehparvar 2006). Thus, no other human rights can be claimed if the nondiscrimination and "do no harm" principle is not applied. It is the principle that makes the other rights operational and, in a sense, makes human rights universal, also in the moral discourse (Zarrehparvar 2006, p. 233).

References

Article 19, Global Campaign for Free Expression. (2010). *Study Paper*. Accessed December 1, 2016, from https://www.article19.org/

DW Akademie. (2015). *Media freedom navigator*. Accessed December 1, 2016, from http://akademie.dw.de/navigator

Zarrehparvar, M. (2006). A nondiscriminatory information society. In R. F. Jorgensen (Ed.), *Human rights in the global information society* (pp. 226–253). Cambridge, MA: MIT Press.

Chapter 4
Public Privacy

"Public privacy" is a notion that aims to describe the dilemma and achievements of promoting and safeguarding freedom rights when using the Internet. The right to privacy and other human rights,[1] such as the right to health, security, freedom of expression, movement, and assembly, or the access to information and education always apply offline as well as online. But in the context of cyberspace, the challenges of safeguarding these entitlements are different and new. Using the Internet allows for anyone to move and communicate, conduct business, and enjoy private life regardless of one's nationality, ethnicity, political orientation, disabilities, gender, or otherwise background to interact on the data highways. Cyberspace offers an environment that seems to have no "natural" borders or limits. Any borders or restrictions we face are man-made and of technological foundation. At the first glance, this space is transparent and neutral by nature. But it is defined, broadened, politicized, limited, and censored by people, companies, organizations, and governments who make use of it. To orientate oneself in this space needs new forms of orientation, education, and technological literacy that most of the four billion users currently still have to learn and understand. On the one hand, we think we act anonymous or only in circles of "our friends" when using private platforms, password protected services, or social media, but at the same time we leave data trails that can be shared with a worldwide public of four billion users at any time if the data is wrongfully protected, sold, or hacked. In most cases, the utilization of our data by others remains unknown to us. It is in a way a schizophrenic situation, because we tend to manage our most private data, such as health insurance, bank accounts, love affairs, and family pictures in "clouds" and password-protected social environments assuming that they are not accessible to others, and at the same time we make this data public. We thus attain to create a sphere of public

---

[1] A good overview over the range of human rights affected specifically through the Internet is given in R. F. Jorgensen (ed.) (2006). Human rights in the global information society. Cambridge, Massachusets: MIT Press.

A. Mihr, *Cyber Justice*, SpringerBriefs in Political Science,
DOI 10.1007/978-3-319-60093-2_4

privacy which allows us to control our data at any time and only allow others to seek this data when we give our consent. But to monitor and control consistent with human rights and good governance principles would need independent global monitoring bodies that vigilante behavior and misconduct.

Bearing this in mind, why then do we share some of our most private and personal data with the global community of millions of personally unknown people? The fact that most of this community and audience of our data is anonymous leaves us in the illusion of a privacy that is different from the one behind apartment walls. However irritating that may be, in the context of human rights, the "right to privacy" is thus one of the key issues to be discussed when promoting human rights in and through the Internet. Privacy rights thus also encompass safety and security rights but also rules for participation which are already enshrined in the most important UN and regional human rights treaties, such as in Art 7 and Art 8 of the EU Charta for Fundamental Rights from 2000. Respect for privacy in connection to data protection is defined as private and family life in which everyone has the right to be respected for his or her private and family life, home, and communications. Everyone has the right to the protection of personal data concerning him or her. Such data must be processed fairly for specified purposes and on the basis of the consent of the person concerned or some other legitimate basis laid down by law. Everyone has the right of access to data that is to say to information, which has been collected concerning him or her, and the right to have it rectified. The novelty in the EU Charter was that these human rights enjoy legal protection through an international Court, the ECJ, and domestic jurisdiction within the EU and beyond, if the case concerned is related to a EU-based server or provider (European Union 2000). To develop our personality in a confident and free way and exercise our skills and capacities, maintain our health, and enjoy social relationships with family and friends in the online world require different skills to uphold, but not different rights (Nissenbaum 1997). Hence, privacy in the cyberspace means using the Internet as a service tool for private purposes without fearing that third parties, such as governments or companies (i.e., national intelligence agencies, Google+, or Microsoft), are accessing, selling, or publically posting our data for security or business purposes without our consent.

By sharing private information to an unknown public, a potential hacker, banks, insurance companies, and so on, Internet users have already created virtual twins in this new space without having ever a chance to delete the information—as burning a piece of paper on which very private and personal information has been written and of which there exists no copy. Personal relationships and "being friends" through social networks, such as Renren and Facebook, can be anonymous on the one side and yet provides a vast amount of personal data and private messages. Digital footprints will lead the way to our private data "home." Today, millions of uprooted people, migrants, and refugees seek a better and more secure life somewhere else, using social media, in particular Facebook, as their often only means of communication and orientations to find their destinations. They leave data trails that for immigration officers and asylum cases in front of courts have often unforeseen negative consequences that are not negotiable. But whereas privacy has already made its way to the cyber public and into governmental offices and commercials, the question remains on how to gain our privacy back and how to avoid massive harm.

With the upcoming of good governance principles in the 1990s as a means to open doors for democratic movements around the world, the Internet became a blessing for the claims of citizens for more transparency of governmental actions and companies' activities. What is private and what is public became blurry at the same time. We learned that we can sell and buy privacy in form of the new currency in cyberspace: our data. The new dollar is the "byte," our data. With "bytes" we pay assumingly "free online services," namely, those services that are free of charge, such as Google, Facebook, Alibaba, WhatsApp, or Amazon. The difference to the common hard currency is that we have no full control over the product we pay with our "money" and thus about our "capital" in this cyber world. Algorithms are determining our expenditures, budgets, and our "bank account" and decide where and how we "shop." In other words, we buy something and give our consent by pressing "confirm" buttons on any website, but by doing this, we automatically have made our data available for public use by everyone. We do need a data-control agency, similar to a revenue or fiscal authority of countries to control the "byte" and money transfer and flow. Today, the cyberspace is like an "illicit financial" market for our data, in which we have no idea in which pockets our data goes.

Yet, as illustrated with this example, black markets and illicit financial flows are nothing new on the planet, but the point is how to gain the control over our accounts and data and thus balance our freedom to move and to decide what happens with our data with the rights of our privacy and principles of transparency and free movement.

Data that is acquired through businesses and enterprises, education and training, finances and economics, private correspondence, and even health and personal issues are now dealt with by anyone who seeks access to it in this "endless" space (Kiskis 2011). The main vehicle, device, or tool by which information moves in this cyberspace remains the Internet that allows for our data to move on the World Wide Web highway with no speed control. But seemingly to national road control and territory, the way people and actors behave and make decisions in this space is guided through principles and norms—a kind of traffic control agency—usually written down in constitutions or laws and in international human rights conventions. Ideally these rules, regulations, and laws are set up by the citizens for the citizens or users for users. That process of setting up common and joint rules and standards by Internet users for Internet users has not taken place properly in cyberspace yet, although organizations such as the UN IGF claim to find multistakeholder-based global solutions. This solution includes consulting governments, CSOs, businesses, and service providers for their advice. In 2013, the IGF meeting in Indonesia confirmed that the way ahead in making the Internet an inclusive tool for all in the future would be the multistakeholder approach (Internet Governance Forum 2013). The IGF has no formal membership and is open to different stakeholders with a demonstrated interest in Internet governance. The consultative Multistakeholder Advisory Group (MAG) to the IGF, with 56 members of various backgrounds, private, corporate, or government, has the mandate to advise the UN on the content and the schedule of the IGF (Internet Governance Forum 2017). The International Telecommunications Union (ITU) is one of the leading organizations managing the encounterment and monitoring that the membership in the MAG is open to various stakeholders (Internet Government Forum 2014). Until 2015, the IGF has largely focused its meetings on security threats on the Internet, such as cyber war and cyber espionage and, thus, on how to deal and control these developments. The agenda of these meetings were set by governments and their interests, which in recent years is no longer the case. The number of NGOs, CSOs, and corporate enterprises which participate in the forum has dramatically increased from a few docents to several hundreds today. However, many of these NGOs or corporates predominantly act (and see their own role) as lobbyists that advocate for a particular cause; others are connected to university research centers or think tanks and issue policy briefs and recommendations, but they do not necessarily take part in the decision-making process or are equally held accountable as state institutions could be in the case of cybercrime or human rights abuses on the Internet. To mention but a few of the institutions that research in this subject matter: the Freeman Spogli Institute at University of Stanford, the Center for Internet and Human Rights at Viadrina University, the Center for Internet Society in India, Freedom House, the Alexander von Humboldt Institute for Internet in Berlin, Transparency International, Amnesty International, and many others. Other than state officials, researchers, NGO staff, and CSO members often work voluntarily or are engaged with other professional commitments. The double commitments and engagement of researchers and volunteers often impair equal participation. True multistakeholder realization is a slow process for many of these nonstate actors when attaining equal participation. In order to do that, NGOs and enterprises alike need to leave their personal or corporate interests behind and open up for those of the general public policy making, which implies short, medium, and long-term engagement in order to take decisions adequately. The recent efforts to allow for the multistakeholder approach to flourish and to move away from the traditional advocacy coalitions to true stakeholder participation and to be on equal footing with governmental actors are slow, as Julia Pohle has assessed. The approach has led, if at all, to more collaboration still "under" the lead of governments in public policy making. Pohle argues that the governance of the Internet is understood as the process of reflexive coordination through which actors question and redefine the rules of the game. And the main actors in this game remain governmental ones. Social order or a social contract between users, companies, governments, and civil society was only partially achieved because none of the proposals and ideas of multistakeholder global governance was institutionalized (yet) through inscription in a consensual text for formal policy recommendations (Pohle 2016, p. 11).

Thus, the multistakeholder process to resolve the dilemma of "public privacy" instead leads to a fragmentation of different sectors that move and deal with cyberspace and Internet: companies and service providers, governments and international organizations, and Internet users and their organizational networks and NGOs. At the IGF or ITUs, they come together, discuss, agree, and disagree, but the final decisions remain to be taken by governments and their legislative powers. Although they act internationally and globally on the level of the UN or EU, it remains to be in governmental hands if Internet policies are decided upon.

Nevertheless, the joint interest in the growth and development of the Internet are inseparable from their recognition of the need for a fair, transparent, and equitable policy process. While previous IGFs have primarily focused on the technical and policy aspects of Internet governance, the 2013 IGF incorporated themes such as human rights, cross-sector cooperation, neutral access, diversity in the Internet, and first claims for a neutral Internet.

And since 2015, it focuses on how to uphold human rights and code of conducts online (Internet Governance Forum 2016). But because the human rights-based approach in the offline worlds is still facing major challenges and obstacles, the online approach does too. It would be an illusion to believe that human rights are better protected in the online world than in the offline one as long as governments do not manage to uphold and safeguard our privacy and freedoms in the offline world; they are hardly to be expected to do better in the online world. There is no better online world than there is an offline one. The key point is the lack of a global cyber and Internet governance regime that allows for implementation and enforcement of human rights in the Internet. Thus, the online world only mirrors our successes or failures to implement human rights in the offline world with the consequence that our data and privacy remains partly uncontrolled and thus unwillingly public.

Since the launch of the Universal Declaration for Human Rights (UDHR) in 1948, and its subsequent covenants and conventions, we have sought over 60 years of experience to uphold these standards through domestic—and sometimes international—jurisdiction, but thus far never managed to fully implement these rights in the offline world (Universal Declaration of Human Rights 1948). International and regional approaches have often been insufficient but also indispensable, such as the Inter-American Court for Human Rights in Costa Rica or the European Court for Human Rights in Strasbourg and other regional regimes (International Justice Resource Center 2017). But despite the offline insufficiency and the increasing challenges and demands from the online world, the global human rights regime aims to respond to the current developments. Some of the normative legal and political frameworks that have successfully proven to protect human rights offline—including regional and domestic jurisdiction—and which we find within state borders mainly in democratic countries could also be transferred to the cyberspace. For example, human rights-related claims procedures, code of conducts, fair trails, penalties, and limitations based on rule of law and others.

Ultimately, what is missing in cyberspace is a quasi-government or cyber-governance regime based on good governance principles, as indicated by the UN, that allow to govern the needs and claims of its citizens through monitoring and enforcement bodies (Council of Europe 2017; United Nations Economic and Social Commission for Asia and the Pacific 2009). These would include effective monitoring and decision-making bodies, independent enforcement mechanisms, and broad and continuous participation of users and businesses in this process. All actors regularly advise, revise, and consult with and respond to each other. In the case of cyberspace, these CSOs or CEOs are Internet users and service providers at the same time.

Thus, the rising phenomenon of "public privacy" encompasses the respect for human rights and fundamental freedoms on the one side and the quest for more protection of our data on the other side. The multistakeholder approach is one of many to negotiate modes of governance to respond to this quest. How to maintain the freedom of information and expression in the Internet and maximum security and privacy on the other side in the cyberspace?

Freedom rights (of movement, assembly, participation, expression, information, and others) are stated in a plethora of international treaties and agreements (United Nations Human Rights Office of the High Commissioner 2017). It encompasses the right of free expression, which includes the freedom to hold opinions and to receive and impart information and ideas without state interference. This right also includes the right to communicate and to express oneself in any medium, including through words, pictures, images, and actions including exchanging ideas and thoughts through social networks or other Internet platforms, to protest against misconduct, and to demonstrate. Freedom means the right to political expression including comments on matters of general public interest, artistic expression, and commercial expression, particularly when it also raises matters of legitimate public debate and concern. Because most democratic countries foster the installment of Internet for market economic reasons and better communication, political expression is given particular precedence and protection. To ensure that free expression and debate is possible, there must be protection for elements of a free and neutral Internet and media such as printed and online press, including protection of journalistic or investigative sources (Mihr 2013).

To uphold freedom and privacy rights on the Internet is a fundamental challenge in times of cyber terror and war. Cyber security, cyber surveillance, and cyber viruses are just a few terminologies that pose fear and a sense of threat to our daily use of the Internet. Some already call it the *World Wide War* in which various actors, such as states and nonstate actors, hackers, terrorist, warlords, and users, are equally involved. These military terms and notions of cyber, as Wagner and Kilian have phrased it earlier, have their roots in the 1980s, but still illustrate that many of us view the cyberspace as a hostile and anarchial environment that needs "civilization" by means of arms and military control. Whether this is the only way ahead is massively questioned by CSOs who foster a peaceful way to govern the cyberspace, namely, through the multistakeholder approach. Commercial state or intergovernmental agreements like SOPA, PRISM, PIPA, or ACTA[2] are just a few international governmental initiatives to regain the control over the borderless dataflow. They aim to control the access to data. Although governments of

[2]See also Better World Links (2017), 'INTERNET Freedom – Privacy, Censorship, SOPA, PIPA & ACTA, CISPA & PRISM', http://www.betterworldlinks.org/index.php?cat=8595. Accessed 19 April 2014.

Singapore, Germany, or Brazil strive for better data protection, these intergovernmental agreements can lead to massive misuse and abuse of private data and turn into censorship by and through national intelligence agencies or private agents such as global "cybersecurity police." Some might ask that if there is a security risk, whether the idea of a "cyber insurance," may it be private or public, would be a way to face the increasing threats and breach of private data on the Internet. An insurance that would protect our data from being misused for reasons other than authorized by us, or cover for our expenses when fighting criminal acts in reference to our data? Such a thrive to "safer space" in cyberspace ought to be benchmarked against human rights and how they can be fully guaranteed under these arrangements. The complete absence of effective data protection will have repercussions and consequences both in leveraging human right realization and in preventing people from enjoying human rights.

Introducing social bots in the battle about control over cyberspace are yet another form of interventions. Bots are algorithm-based programs that act as "human robots" on the Internet and aim to maneuver, intervene, moderate, or simply manipulate public opinions and "Likes." These bots filter information and provide our own "privacy bubble or echo-chamber" on our private Facebook, WhatsApp, Instagram, or Twitter accounts. Our private Internet or e-mail account has all become a public subject of social bots in one way or the other. These bots provide us with data, commercials, propaganda, information, or news that influence our opinion, voting, consumer, and shopping behavior. They are our "algorithm mindset" that orchestrate our minds in what we believe that we need or want—whether it is based on factual needs and truth or not. Used strategically in election campaigns in the USA and in Europe since 2016, these bots maneuver our minds and voting habits toward specific results. They shape our opinion and thus enter in our most private lives—our consciousness in a way that seems to be uncontrollable and beyond our rational minds. Although campaigning, advertising, and propaganda are far from being anything of only modern times, Ferrara et al. (2015) argue that these social bots are different from the usual campaigning or propaganda. Bots are artificial intelligence tools and can interact, often unnoticed, with real people in social media ecosystems. They are helpful tools in the health or agricultural sectors when allocating data that allows for timely prognosis that humans cannot provide. But whereas human campaigners are somewhat obvious and transparent, while following a human logic, social bots' algorithms follow their own logic that is not necessarily based on human or community behavior. Whether they really seek to improve the common well and weal, the *Gemeinwohl*, is rather doubtful and not proven yet. Their abundance and dynamic is uncertain and uncontrollable in cyberspace, because once they are programmed, there are no sights of tiredness, human limits, or physical borders; they produce data, allocate, and disseminate—regardless of the counterparts feelings, socioeconomic background, or otherwise personal situation. Although some bots are helpful tools to allocate data and provide forecasts, others can be harmful bots with the goals of persuading, smearing, or deceiving people, politics, business, and thus massively interfere in the *Gemeinwohl* of a whole society. It becomes even more dramatic if we consider the fact that these bots develop their own dynamic and cannot be stopped. Modern, sophisticated social bots and their presence can endanger online ecosystems and our society, for example, through Twitter. Common patterns of generating information and making a rational assessment, making up our minds, and deciding whom we want to vote for in elections and how we are imitated by bots seem yet beyond our imagination. Because they can help discriminate synthetic behaviors from human ones, yielding signatures of engineered social tampering and otherwise impact our human behavior and social interaction (Ferrara et al. 2015). Thus, even despite all innovations in and for the Internet, the challenge again remains that of the control and governance of cyberspace.

The consequences of social bots illustrate that social behavior and interaction is the foundation of any of our privacy, may it be family based or concerning our very own skills and capacities as well as health or other private issues. Social bots and humans need to be able to recognize each other, to avoid bizarre, or even dangerous, situations based on false assumptions of human interlocutors and, thus, keep our judgments and data as untouched from these unhuman algorithms as possible. For this to be achieved, it needs a global public governance and policy agreement.

References

Council of Europe. (2017). *The 12 principles for good governance at local level, with tools for implementation*. Accessed April 1, 2017, from http://www.coe.int/t/dgap/localdemocracy/Strategy_Innovation/12principles_en.asp

European Union. (2000, December 18). *Charter of Fundamental Rights of the European Union*.

Ferrara, E., Varol, O., Davis, C., Menczer, F., & Flammini, A. (2015). *The rise of social bots*. Accessed April 1, 2017, from doi:10.1145/0000000.0000000.

International Justice Resource Center. (2017). *Regional systems*. Accessed April 1, 2017, from http://www.ijrcenter.org/regional/

Internet Governance Forum. (2013). *IGF 2013*. Accessed April 1, 2017, from http://www.intgovforum.org/cms/2013-bali

Internet Government Forum. (2014). *Building bridges: Enhancing multistakeholder cooperation for growth and sustainable development*. Accessed April 1, 2017, from http://www.intgovforum.org/multilingual/filedepot_download/3367/11

Internet Governance Forum. (2016). *The Internet Governance Forum*. Accessed April 1, 2017, from http://www.intgovforum.org/

Internet Governance Forum. (2017). *The Multistakeholder Advisory Group: MAG eligibility criteria for funding a participant*. Accessed April 1, 2017, from http://www.intgovforum.org/cms/mag

Kiskis, M. (2011). Entrepreneurship in cyberspace: What do we know? *Mykolas Romeris University, 1*(1), 37–48. Accessed April 1, 2017, from https://papers.ssrn.com/sol3/papers.cfm?abstract_id=1954553

Mihr, A. (2013). Public Privacy: Human Rights in Cyberspace, SIM Working Paper, Utrecht University, December 2013. http://www.anjamihr.com/resources/Public+Privacy-WP-AnjaMihr 5D.pdf

Nissenbaum, H. (1997). Toward an approach to privacy in public: Challenges of information technology. *Ethics & Behaviour*, *7*(3), 207–219. Accessed April 1, 2017, from http://www.nyu.edu/projects/nissenbaum/papers/toward_an_approach.pdf

Pohle, J. (2016). Multistakeholder governance processes as production sites: Enhanced cooperation "in the making". *Internet Policy Review, Journal on Internet Regulation*, *5*(3).
Universal Declaration of Human Rights, United Nations. (1948, December 10).
United Nations Economic and Social Commission for Asia and the Pacific. (2009). *What is good governance?* Accessed April 1, 2017, from http://www.unescap.org/sites/default/files/good-governance.pdf
United Nations Human Rights Office of the High Commissioner. (2017). *Universal human rights index database*. Accessed April 1, 2017, from http://www.ohchr.org/EN/HRBodies/Pages/UniversalHumanRightsIndexDatabase.aspx

Chapter 5
Justice

Justice in the words of John Rawls is a concept of fairness based on liberty of and equality among people, providing that people are free and capacitated enough to use their rational minds and take decisions that benefit the whole society in short-, medium-, and long-term developments (Rawls 1985). To remain a free, self-conscious, self-determined, and rational Internet user that we all think we are, Rawls' justice concept could be translated into one of cyber justice. Justice in a cyberspace in which people move and act, use it, and participate freely, almost unlimited, with equal access to information, services by free participation, and expression through the use of web-based technology is an idea that primarily intrigued the use of the Internet in the first place (Mihr 2016, p. 321).

That could be all true—in an ideal world—if it were not for the possibility of some Internet providers to censor, manipulate, breach, and misuse our access to information through social bots or other form of algorithm-based programs that filter, manipulate, and generate data. Whereas we do not want to prejudge over people's intentions, we can observe that there is a lack of global and independent institutions and agencies that could regulate and control the way these liberties are executed (Colomer 2014). Instead the data trail we leave in cyberspace is used, censored, and manipulated. And the way it is done impacts our equal, free, and neutral access to basic resources in the Internet. Cyber justice would mean to allow for free and neutral access to these resources without harming one's privacy and integrity. Some would call it dignity.

In 2010, the University of Montreal in Canada launched the cyber justice laboratory aiming to solve legal problems online rather than offline for communities that lack a good and independent functioning legal system in their country or district. The university researchers aimed to overcome the shortage of rule of law in some parts of the world by means of information technology, filling the gap between local injustice and denial of law, and global human rights and law standards. It aimed to bring to these communities global legal protection mechanism in the area of criminal law. In their justice laboratory, they aimed for a close cooperation with all stakeholders, the defendant, the lawyers or judges, and the

A. Mihr, *Cyber Justice*, SpringerBriefs in Political Science,
DOI 10.1007/978-3-319-60093-2_5

government or CSOs, in any particular case (Cyberjustice Laboratory 2016). The Internet was a tool to bring justice to people, but not the other way around. Nevertheless, the pilot projects confirmed that rules, norms, and law can be successfully executed via the Internet and thus the physical presence of judges or courtrooms is not a prerequisite to bring about justice. Online consultancy, education, and treatment of various kinds have long been a common practice in many public sectors. But in the context of criminal justice, for example, these approaches are still rare and face major obstacles when protecting witnesses, interrogation practices, keeping the accused in detention, or seeking testimonials.

Thus, justice in cyberspace is a public and common endeavor rather than a technical one. Free expression of belief, political opinion, exercising art and written texts, safety and security of the individual, free and equal access to information, and the protection of privacy issues such as family relations, friendships, or health issues are basic to uphold justice. To be free from harassment and persecution, "shitstorms," and hate speech while enjoying one's own political, ethical, or gender identity is hard to balance anywhere. Justice in cyberspace has to protect one's own intellectual property and creativity, for example, art, movies, pictures, literature, and scientific results, as well as having access at any time to fair and open trials. But one step is to assess what this notion of justice is in the context of the *Gemeinwohl*, and the other step is to reach it.

The often proclaimed "right to Internet" or a "Digital Rights Charta" aims to frame justice in cyberspace. These claims by policy makers and Internet users (mostly in the Global South) aim for neutral, equal, and at the same time protected access to the Internet. As illustrated earlier, the "right to be forgotten," which assures that one's own private data remains private and can be deleted at any time, is already part of the overall global human rights framework, namely, via the "right to privacy and data protection" (as in the EU Fundamental Rights Charta). Thus, in normative terms, there is no need for a new international convention with specific Internet-related human rights. Starting in 2016, Facebook's worldwide campaign to inform their users about the fact that they can delete posts and "be forgotten" aimed at winning back trust and confidence among their users and customers, followed by Google in 2017 launching a public campaign on privacy in the Internet, both in paper as well as virtual form.[1] These campaigns are self-imposed "vetting" procedures with the aim to delete inadequate and compromising data from personal pages, blogs, or social networks that would harm people's dignity or development in the short, medium, and long run. Despite the honorable effort to do so, private companies such as Facebook or Google, Yahoo, or WhatsApp have their own "human rights benchmarks" to do it and, thus, these vetting procedures are not reliable let alone according to international human rights standards. But the fact that these companies reacted to the public pressure to change their commercial policies and to protect more human rights, not

[1]Google Privacy and Data Protection campaign https://www.google.com/takeaction (Accessed 21 April 2017).

less, are a first step toward a corporate social responsibility agreement between users and companies.

Moreover, the recent developments in the corporate sector mirrors the distrustful and suspicious interrelationship between individuals and the services provided through the Internet. Much of this distrust emerged out of the misuse of data by companies. It leads to self-censorship by users not posting information of a private character on the Internet or not posting any information at all—with negative consequences for the user him/herself. The "delete," "forgetting"—security-campaign by Facebook would have been needless if the largest social network in the world would have protected the privacy rights of its customers in the first place. Global standards and transparent information of what is seen as private and what is categorized as public data would have helped to retain trust by users. Private data ought not to be passed on without consent. This should have been a corporate policy by the company before Facebook even started to go online in 2004. Thus, the company deliberately violated human rights of its customers. It started to protect them when trust in and use of its services stagnated and decreased around the year 2015. But could there have been another policy in the first place? Is the current debate on how much freedom and how much restrictions on the Internet we can bear a normal evolution of the process in defining cyber justice? Kieron O'Hara (2005) opts for the latter and argues that the rights-based discourse favored by philosophers such as John Rawls about what privileges and restrictions people should have when exercising their freedoms becomes a global public policy issue. Since cyberspace concerns almost half of the world's population, the issue about how to exercise our freedoms is ripe for debate. O'Hara finds compromises essential in order to allow access for users from the Global South, in particular from the growing number of young and nonwealthy users to negotiations over how to promote cyber trust, for example, when discussing the possibilities of neutral, nonprofit, and commonly owned Internet. These negotiations may be messy and complex because the problem is that many of the globally dispersed alternative political cultures find the trade-off between privacy and security much less difficult than do most Western liberal societies. Thus, O'Hara raises the point that these trade-offs might drag the Internet further away from the anarchistic ideals of its founding fathers into a security-based cyber governance regime in which neutrality is actually at stake (O'Hara 2005, p. 448). It would well be that search engines and social networks, that make profit by the use of our data, will ask governments and tax payers to pay them compensations in exchange for providing neutral and nonprofit services to Internet users in poorer regions of the world.

But even though making a deal with profit-based companies who thus far call almost 100% of the cyberspace their own, the question of justice remains open. Case law as such on Facebook or Google in recent years will most likely take quite some time to establish interpretations of these rights. The research division of the ECtHR has already in 2011 published groundbreaking documents on the potential of the case law concerning data protection and retention issues relevant for the Internet could mean in future decisions taken by the Court. In this document, the freedom of expression, intellectual property, and issues of cybercrime are seen as major deficits that yet have to be further defined and interpreted through case law (European Court of Human Rights and Council of Europe 2011). Further below, I will give two examples of recent cases ruled by the Court in 2012 and 2013 under these provisions.

As a consequence, universal basic human rights principles and norms remain the only benchmark when seeking justice in cyberspace. This was already reconfirmed in 1993 during the World Conference for Human Rights in Vienna, Austria (UN - Secretary-General 1993). Whether fundamental freedoms and human rights are universal or not are therefore no longer an issue of intergovernmental debates (as they had been for the whole duration of the Cold War from 1945 to 1990) but rather a question of how to implement and enforce these rights into national legislation. During the 1993 conference, all UN member states confirmed that all human rights derive from the dignity and worth inherent in the human person. The individual person is the central subject of human rights and fundamental freedoms, and consequently s/he should be the principal beneficiary and should participate actively in the realization of these rights and freedoms (United Nations Human Rights Office of the High Commissioner 1993). That is applied to today's Internet user as it does to the person walking on the street. According to this statement, human rights are entitlements inherent to all human beings, regardless of nationality, place of residence, sex, national or ethnic origin, color, religion, language, or any other status. We are equally entitled to the protection and promotion of these human rights without discrimination. Human rights are interrelated, interdependent, and indivisible and embrace sets of different values such as solidarity, confidentiality, fairness, or friendship as well as principles, norms, and standards such as the right to fair trial, the freedom of expression, the right to adequate housing, access to water, or access to information.

Yet, apart from the general renewal and agreement in 1993, the question remains on how to implement them in the online world. Most of the international human rights law and treaties have turned into customary international law and became general principles that frame attitudes and behavior of state and nonstate actors as well as companies (UN Doc. General Assembly Resolution 217 A (III). Preamble of the Universal Declaration of Human Rights 1948). They include obligations and duties of governments, companies, individuals, or other legal entities (duty-bearers) to act in certain ways or to refrain from certain acts. Duty-bearers, such as governments, but also companies and service providers, such as Facebook, Amazon, E-bay, PayPal, or Google, have to respect and protect human rights of right holders. If they violate them, they must be held accountable for it. That is to say that any person and citizen on this planet, regardless of his or her background, can claim these rights in front of local or national, and if possible, international or regional courts. But if the violator of these rights is a service provider not legally registered in the country of the users' residence, the international public and treaty law (a jurisdiction that aims to regulate disputes among countries and customers between different countries) comes soon to its limits. There is no global cyber or Internet court (yet) that would regulate our disputes with private companies when they violate our human rights in cyberspace.

At the same time, the claims for justice in the online world rise. They are phrased as social, civil, economic, political, or cultural justice, and there is no hierarchy between them. Social human rights are, for example, the right to education, health, social security, family, and marriage. Civil rights are those to participate, to assemble, to live in dignity, to enjoy fair and open trial, to be free from torture, and to enjoy physical integrity. Economic human rights are those to work, to get adequate salary, to enjoy holidays, and to set up enterprises. Political rights are those to vote or be elected, to participate in decision-making processes, and so on. Cultural rights are those to religious freedom and practice as well as customs and traditions (Alston 2006). Eventually, all these different categories of human rights cannot be exercised or enjoyed without one another and in our online world. They come together in a way and with a paste they did not necessarily do so earlier. The right to housing or to work, the freedom of religion, or the right to health can only be enjoyed or pressed for if the human rights to assemble, protest, and participate allow us to make open claims for these rights in case they are not executed or respected. Protests and insults, hate speech, allegations, and serious claims and concerns about the violation or disregard of these rights are now transmitted in seconds around the world and sometimes leave little to no time for investigation or clarification. It seems that we have well understood our role as right holders but not yet of duty-bearers at the same time.

This is the holistic approach to human rights under the principle of the earlier mentioned golden rule of "do no harm to others as you would have them to do to you" (Internet Encyclopedia of Philosophy 2010). This means that all these human rights ought to be balanced and estimated insofar as they do not harm the rights of others. The human right to information and data, for example, applies to the extent that this information does not violate the dignity or privacy of others. For example, if my personal data about health or family would be accessible for everyone, it carries the risk that this information violates my privacy and integrity rights. This aspect is often applied when it comes to child pornography on the Internet and similar child abusing images that violate the physical integrity, dignity, and development of the child as such. Both the technical provider and the personal beneficiary of these images are violating the rights of the child and should be held accountable. Companies that provide Internet platforms for private use cannot claim to be nonresponsible for the misuse of the platform. The companies share responsibility. This is similar to the official status of the weapon industry that is subject to governmental limits and laws regarding the aspect to which countries they can legally sell their weapons and arms. Of course, laws and governmental control does not avoid abuse or illegal trade at the end, but it clearly formulates responsibilities and accountabilities.

The overall benchmark for accountability is when human rights are violated and when other people's dignity and integrity is harmed. Regardless of who is the beneficiary of it, a private or public entity, they ought to be held accountable. Whereas this is not much disputed, the problem remains that even if we know the companies or persons behind the violations, we cannot necessarily hold them accountable because of the lack of legislation, police, or courts that deal with issues of human rights violations in cyberspace.

Another slippery slope between freedom and protection begins when we argue that the protection of data should never justify governmental or self-censorship or random surveillance. Prior to any censorship, for example, taking data, films, or pictures off the Internet, it should be explained, based on a human rights-based approach, on what grounds data was retained or a website closed. It is here where the balance starts, and it depends very much on who decides about the limits and borders of freedom to information.

Thus, the third aspect comes in the game: the role of the actors. Who is responsible (the duty-bearer) for taking down images or regulating data? The government, the private service provider, or the user? The more stakeholders are involved, the more complex the situation gets but with an agreed result; it is more likely this balance and result might be accepted by people. This leads to the birth of the multi-stakeholder approach around 2001. At that time, the—still small—international online community agreed on its observation that governments alone, let alone private service providers, cannot and will not guarantee and safeguard our privacy or freedoms on the Internet because the World Wide Web is not a domestic affair but a global one. Thus, a multistakeholder community was needed to include all private and public interests in the debate (Utting 2002).

For example, the right to enjoy scientific progress under the International Covenant on Economic, Social and Cultural Rights (ICESCR)[2] of 1966 specifies in Art 15 that "everyone enjoys the benefits of scientific progress and its applications" on, for example, scientific research and medicine patents or copyrights on technology and art. These rights are valid offline as well as online and it makes therefore no difference whether we illegally copy an artifact in a museum or in cyberspace; both acts are a violation of human rights. In Art 13, for example, the human right to education is mentioned. It means that education should be made accessible, offline as well as online, to capacitate, train, educate, and empower people in order to develop their human personality. They should be empowered to participate in decision-making processes in their professional lives and to govern societies. This right also includes access to online teaching or to E-Governance. Art 17 of the ICCPR from 1966 states that "no one shall be subjected to arbitrary or unlawful interference with his privacy, family, home or correspondence, or to unlawful attacks on his honor and reputation." This article is fundamental for the understanding of the protection of our freedom and privacy rights in cyberspace because in this article we read further that everyone has the right to the protection of the law against such interference or attacks. Most liberty and freedom rights can be found in this Covenant as well as in other international human rights treaties in Africa, Europe, the Arab world, or the Americas; for example, Art 3 establishes the nondiscrimination principle, Art 18 mandates freedom of religion, Art 19 upholds

[2]These human rights are expressed in major international treaties, such as the ICCPR and the ICESCR 1966.

the freedom of expression, Art 20 mandates sanctions against inciting hatred, Articles 21 and 22 mandate freedom of association, and so on.

All these human rights, to name but a few, are internationally recognized, and even though some countries have not ratified these covenants, most of these rights have turned into customary international human rights law. This means that even if countries have not ratified certain international treaties, the internationally recognized human rights are generally valid and applicable even without the consent of a government, for example, within national jurisdiction. They are customary and general because the majority of countries—and assumingly people—around the world adhere or include aspects of them in their national legislation or legal procedures.

Following the controversies on justice in the context of cybersecurity and national sovereignty versus the individual freedoms of users over the past decades, in 2011, the UN Special Rapporteur on Freedom of Expression, Frank de la Rue from Guatemala, urged governments not to cut off users from Internet access, regardless of the justification provided, including on the grounds of violating intellectual property rights law, to be disproportionate, and thus a violation of article 19, paragraph 3, of the ICCPR. He called upon all states to ensure that Internet access is maintained at all times, including during times of political unrest (La Rue 2011, para 23, 79). And in 2012, the UN Human Rights Council in Geneva reconfirmed that the same rights that people have offline must also be protected online, and it called upon its member states to ensure freedom of expression and the access to Internet, for example, the access to international cooperations that provide media information such as social networks, search engines, etc. (UN General Assembly 2012).

In 2013, during a number of occasions and events on the international and national level, such as the National Security Agency (NSA) affair between the USA, Germany, and Brazil, the issues of cyber espionage and misuse of private data became public. In consequence and response to these different developments and incidents, the UN Special Rapporteur de la Rue once again urged the UN member states to ensure that individuals are able to freely seek and receive information or express themselves while respecting, protecting, and promoting their right to privacy. He highlighted the fact that privacy and freedom of expression are interlinked and mutually dependent and therefore without adequate legislation and legal standards to ensure the privacy, security, and anonymity of communications, journalists, HRD, and whistleblowers cannot be assured that their communications will not be subject to states' security (La Rue 2013, para 79). The UN report received many responses, in particular by the civil society organizations (CSO) network community. CSOs have long claimed that human rights are not protected well enough in cyberspace. The Electronic Frontier Foundation (EFF), for example, claimed that technologies can open a Pandora's box of previously unimaginable state surveillance intrusions, and metadata can reveal sensitive information that can be easily accessed, stored, mined, and exploited (Electronic Frontier Foundation 2013).

Hence, so far there is no regional or international human rights regime within or under the UN, ASEAN, EU, OSCE, OAS, or AU that is adequately equipped and installed to deal with the consequences and effects of global flow of data, intellectual property, secret information, or private data, even though all these regimes have the topic on their agendas. Although citizens that use the Internet within the borders of regional organizations, such as the EU, enjoy some protection, these measures are not valid globally. The USA and China have long urged for joint binding agreements to deal with the borderless data flow in order to either protect or to restrict the use of the Internet. But altogether, they have the same goal to control cyberspace and subsequently the Internet. In technical terms, it can be compared with the fight with windmills that cannot be won by state institutions nor by international intergovernmental regimes alone. It needs more to control the wind and the air, and solutions are anything but local. The reason why it takes more than just a few governments in international regimes, such as the UN or the EU, to solve the problems is that it takes effective global and neutral institutions to enforce common rules. Without the wider cybercommunity, like technical companies, Internet providers, or search engines, and so on, effective enforcement mechanism will less likely be established. Because the cyberspace is not restricted to states or to any geographical or physical borders, it is thus not bound to any state or inter-state agreement and cannot to be controlled by state institutions alone.

The international human rights regime, for example, is entirely based on states' (often nonbinding) willingness and capacity to promote and protect human rights and is therefore a valid but weak institutional setup to govern cyberspace. Moreover, because this international regime depends on the joint agreements and regulations set by governments, including democratic and nondemocratic ones, such as Russia, Brazil, Nigeria, USA, Germany, or China, the results are often compromises that lack strong monitoring and enforcement mechanisms based on international human rights law. More so, other stakeholders are often excluded from this process, for example, Internet service providers, let alone the global network community or the billions of individual users, namely, us. And thus, the UN IGF, based on national institutions and their agencies and delegates, also remains mainly a governmental institution with strong nongovernmental participation. It is not truly transnational, although it aims to solve transnational violations of human rights and privacy.

References

Alston, P. (2006). Reconceiving the UN human rights regime, challenges confronting the new UN Human Rights Council. *Melbourne Journal of International Law, 7*(1.) Accessed January 1, 2017, from http://www5.austlii.edu.au/au/journals/MelbJIL/2006/9.html.

Colomer, J. M. (2014). *How global institutions rule the world*. Basingstoke: Palgrave Macmillian.

Cyberjustice Laboratory. (2016). Accessed January 1, 2017, from http://www.cyberjustice.ca/en/projets/vers-la-cyberjustice/

Electronic Frontier Foundation. (2013). *Internet surveillance and free speech: The United Nations makes the connection*. Accessed January 1, 2017, from https://www.eff.org/deeplinks/2013/06/internet-and-surveillance-UN-makes-the-connection

European Court of Human Rights & Council of Europe. (2011). *Internet: Case-law of the European Court of Human Rights*. Accessed January 1, 2017, from www.echr.coe.int

Internet Encyclopedia of Philosophy. (2010). *The golden rule*. Accessed January 1, 2017, from http://www.iep.utm.edu/goldrule/

La Rue, F. (2011, May 16). *Report of the special rapporteur on the promotion and protection of the right to freedom of opinion and expression: A/HRC/17/27*.

La Rue, F. (2013, April 17). *Report of the special rapporteur on the promotion and protection of the right to freedom of opinion, and expression, Frank La Rue: UN Doc. A/HRC/17/27*.

Mihr, A. (2016). Cyber justice: Cyber-governance through human rights and a rule of law in the internet. *US-China Law Review, 13*(4), 314–336.

O'Hara, K. (2005). The ethics of cyber trust. In R. Mansell, & B. S. Collins (Eds.), *Trust and crime in information societies* (pp. 442–449). Cheltenham: Edward Elgar.

Rawls, J. (1985). Justice as fairness: Political not metaphysical. *Philosophy and Public Affairs, 14*, 223–251.

UN General Assembly. (1948, December 18). *UN Doc. General Assembly Resolution 217 A (III). Preamble of the Universal Declaration of Human Rights*.

UN General Assembly. (2012). *The promotion, protection and enjoyment of human rights on the internet, UN General Assembly. UN Doc. A/HRC/20/L.13*.

UN Secretary-General. (1993). *UN Doc, GA A/CONF.157/24 (Part I): Report of the world conference on human rights*. Accessed January 1, 2017, from http://www.unhchr.ch/Huridocda/Huridoca.nsf/(Symbol)/A.CONF.157.24+(Part+I).En

United Nations Human Rights Office of the High Commissioner. (1993). *World conference on human rights*. Accessed January 1, 2017, from http://www.ohchr.org/EN/AboutUs/Pages/ViennaWC.aspx

Utting, P. (2002). *Regulating business via multistakeholder initiatives: A preliminary assessment*. Accessed January 1, 2017, from http://www.unrisd.org/80256B3C005BCCF9/(httpAuxPages)/35F2BD0379CB6647C1256CE6002B70AA/%24file/uttngls.pdf

Chapter 6
Cyber Law

Currently, there is no specific international or universal cyber law to protect human rights or to combat cyber attacks or the wild and anarchical dissemination of private data and secret files. But it is not a matter of domestic or international jurisdiction, let alone the lack of norms which makes law in cyberspace so challenging, but rather the lack of globally harmonized enforcement mechanisms, such as police and courts. When the ECJ charges Google to withdraw a certain entry from its search engine concerning an EU citizen, it does not mean that Google USA or Indonesia does the same. Thus, the main challenge in cyber law remains enforcement of existing and yet to develop cyber law and human rights. That in return is connected to the main open question on how we will govern the cyberspace in the future?

But with only 8 out of the 100 largest Internet providers coming from Europe (or with headquarters based in Europe), the struggle to hold them accountable via court decisions of the ECJ remains rather limited. The Freedom Online Coalition network, for example, one of the oldest in the field of human rights protection in cyberspace, has launched a number of claims to develop a rule of law in cyberspace (Freedom Online Coalition 2017). The coalition reiterates the fact that we neither need "new" human rights for the Internet nor a "new" rule of law but instead a better coordination of the "different" existing rule of laws and jurisprudences across the world (Internet Jurisdiction 2017). With the rise of cross-border cases of freedom and privacy issues in the context of breach of data, these claims become louder.

Jaqueline Lipton has written one of the most remarkable books on cyber law in this line of argumentation. She highlights that the lack of physical interaction online means that Internet or cyber law—thus far—deals entirely with intangible property issues. All online interactions involve the participation of one or more intermediaries. That is to say organizations that enable digital information exchange such as service providers that offer search engines, online social networks, electronic retailers, data aggregators, blogs, educational institutions, and governmental departments. Therefore, she argues that cyber law is the regulation about the interaction between a third-party mediator, the intermediator with information,

A. Mihr, *Cyber Justice*, SpringerBriefs in Political Science,
DOI 10.1007/978-3-319-60093-2_6

and data exchange (Lipton 2015, pp. 2–3). In short, data versus service providers. What is striking is that throughout her assessment of the legal developments and jurisdiction worldwide, she could not find a lack of domestic or regional jurisdiction, thus no lack of law or rights as such that would apply to the violation of rights or law in cyberspace because these violations are similar to the ones offline. The challenge she describes is how to implement court decisions that are taken in one part of the world to a service provider, such as Google or Facebook, that is located in another part of the world. Furthermore, the challenge is that these providers—although they are legal entities and thus can be held accountable—sometimes use algorithms and other software that have its own dynamics and that cannot be traced back to one specific person or entity. In addition, every country and thus jurisdiction has different norms and standards on how to execute court decision, ranging from issuing penalties to prison sentences, for the same crimes or violations. Harmonization of international law in the areas of capital crimes, trade, human rights, trafficking, arms control, environmental protection, or security—to name but a few issues—has already been a challenge for decades and is nothing new in a rapidly globalizing world. The novelty instead is that the data and actors moving in cyberspace are moving and developing on high speed and often without a clear trace of who has posted or installed what on which server and where. If one website is closed down, it opens up again at a different domain. There are multiple entities, companies, and stakeholders involved, and clear responsibilities are not easy to detect.

Therefore, the main common themes of cyber law revolve around (1) the global reach of the Internet; (2) differing norms of behavior that occur online as compared to those in the physical world, in particular with the rapid increase of hate speech by fake or anonymous identities; and (3) the kinds of harms suffered as a result of undesirable online behavior. Part of this might be the absence of the interaction of physical bodies or facial language and expression and the immediate interaction between people that usually impact conduct in the real world (Lipton 2015, p. 3). There is no such "human filter" in the online world where thoughts and ideas are expressed without awaiting for the general mode, situation, or circumstances or reaction and expressions of others. Instead social bots often imitate human behavior and mislead our reactions toward it. Thus, the only conduct that can impact our online behavior is the "do no harm rule" and the constant assessment of whether an online posting harms or does not harm another person's integrity. In line with Lipton's argumentation, the field of cyber law will consequently involve appropriate legal remedies for the new forms of harms, such as massive hate speech, that occur because of the different dynamics of the Internet communication. Therefore, what might be a major clue to shift from domestic jurisdiction to a global one is to shift from personal jurisdiction to that of an intermediary one. And digital intermediaries responsible for misuse of data or language can be many, for the same crime or violation of human right that occurs because or through the Internet. They can be a CEO of a search engine company or a service provider, a software engineer, and developer of certain algorithm, a social bot (and its programmer) that sends fake messages and manipulates users to focus through micro-targeting of search results on the Internet, the hardware company that provides the facilities, or the customer him or herself using a program or social media service to spread inappropriate language or images that violate the dignity of others. But the first step to reach global jurisdiction for crime and violation commitment in cyberspace is that of harmonization of existing criminal and human rights law in theory and practice. The current lack of domestic jurisdiction on data protection or human rights has led to confusion among users and providers. The lack of cross-border enforcement has led to the temptation of powerful countries to exert political pressure on less powerful ones to bring their law to compliance (Lipton 2015, p. 8), as is the case in the cybercrime battles between the USA and China or the EU and the USA.

Judges often do not agree in creating a new cyber law to protect human rights. They applied common norms and international human rights law to cases concerning cyberspace and therefore guaranteed access to information and communication as a basic human right. Similarly, in a case concerning Turkey in 2012, the ECtHR has reinforced the right of individuals to access the Internet through a ruling against wholesale blocking of online content, asserting that the Internet has now become one of the principal means of exercising the right to freedom of expression and information (European Court of Human Rights 2012, para 54). The judges in Strasbourg ruled on a benchmark case, which established relevance for the arguments against such human rights violations. And in 2013, the same court set yet other groundbreaking standards for the Internet. In October 2013, the ECtHR ruled that an Estonian news portal, Delfi, was responsible for offensive anonymous posts after it had reported about a ferry company. In 2010, Estonia's Supreme Court ruled that the website was responsible for the comments, not the people who made them, and the judges in Strasbourg backed that stance in 2015 (European Court of Human Rights 2015). In consequence that means that service providers, website owners, and others will be held accountable if "their users" or visitors post inadequate language on their websites that violates the dignity and privacy of others or statements that are simply false or impede the progress or development of third parties—as was the case in Estonia. If false allegations or harmful expressions against others appear on the Internet, the owner or provider of the website can be held responsible for it. More of these cases are reported by the Institute for Information Law and other legal monitoring organizations and institutions. Many of them are based at universities and law clinics or cyber justice laboratories, such as at the University of Montreal. They not only observe court cases as pilots, examples, or simply case law but also draw conclusions, such as a list of standards for oversights and transparency of intelligence services, focusing on interception of electronic communications based on good governance and human rights principles (Eskens et al. 2015). Another response to the increasing frauds and crimes in the Internet are NGO and CSO initiatives taking up strategic litigations against governments when they fail to protect freedom rights and secure private data of their citizens in the Internet. The US-based American Civil Liberty Organization or the German-based Gesellschaft für Freiheitsrechte (Association for Freedom Rights) and Digital Courage are just a few examples of initiatives that take national constitutions as their benchmarks to fight massive surveillance, breach of data, and censorship in cyberspace due to a lack of governmental actions in their country. Many of these cases resemble the helplessness and incapability of national policy makers to cooperate transnational to close the legal gap to fight human rights abuses on the Internet.

The conservative definition of cybercrime instead, that is to say using chat rooms, WhatsApp, social networks, or other Internet and e-mail-based communication tools to harm and violate the integrity of others, for example, through cyber mobbing or hate speech, poses a challenge to current jurisdiction, even in a global context. Computer technologies are as such seen as one tool that can abuse human rights. The 2014 annual report by the CoE's "Safer Internet Centers," a joint governmental initiative to report on data abuse related to children and young people, stated that the Center had received 1.5 billion reports and news about illegal content on the Internet, most of them in social media and through social networks. Over half of these reports (57%) were confirmed to be related to child sexual abuse, and 98% of these reports were directly passed on to domestic law enforcement agencies to launch litigations against those who provided the post and content on the Internet (INSAFE-INHOPE Network 2014, p. 7). Thus, it is not to blame the technique as such but how the Internet is used morally, legally, as well as politically to communicate with others.

Apart from the misuse of posting, collecting, selling, or manipulating our data, the most rising aspect of cybercrime is that of hate crime in the Internet that impairs dramatically people's development and dignity in our times. According to the Organization for Security and Cooperation in Europe (OSCE) definition, these web-based hate crimes "are criminal acts committed with a bias motive" (OSCE Office for Democratic Institutions and Human Rights 2014, p. 16). The CoE Convention on Cyber Crime, dating back to 2001, already gives a definition of cybercrimes. In Article 2 of the Convention, it is stated as "criminal offences under its domestic law, when committed intentionally, the access to the whole or any part of a computer system without right" (Convention on Cyber Crime 2001). The CoE Convention focuses on the primary role of member states and state authorities to uphold security and prevent crimes. Each state party may require that the offence be committed by infringing security measures with the intent of obtaining computer data or by other dishonest intent in relation to a computer system that is connected to another computer system. The 47 member states of the Council define crimes in the context of computer technology in Art 1 of the Convention as "any device or a group of interconnected or related devices, one or more of which, pursuant to a program, performs automatic processing of data." This data means any representation of facts, information, or concepts in a form suitable for processing in a computer system, including a program suitable to cause a computer system to perform a function. But the Council goes on and defines service providers, such as Facebook or Google, on the Internet and often the most frequent co-responsible for cybercrimes as "any public or private entity that provides to users of its service the ability to communicate by means of a computer system, and any other entity that processes or stores computer data on behalf of such communication service or users of such service" (Convention on Cyber Crime 2001). The novelty in this Convention was not the fact that breach of data is a crime but the identification of multiple actors that can be held accountable beyond governmental accountability. Since then, the Council focuses not only on national jurisdiction concerning the misuse or breach of data but also on the international one, highlighting that the challenges lay not in the definition of cybercrime but also on the providers. The member states also highlight the need for global cyber jurisdiction when combating these crimes (Council of Europe 2017). The fact that 5 years later, in 2006, the IGF was founded with a clear approach to include multiple-stakeholders shows that the government- or state-centered focus to prevent crimes and uphold security was no longer realistic and enforceable.

It is this motive that makes hate crimes, such as hate postings and "shitstorms," different from other crimes such as breach of big data, mega data, or personal data. We send messages, check our bank account, read social media, order products, send e-mails, put pictures and data on Dropbox, pay online bills, watch movies online, chat and Skype online, and thus produce tons of data on an hourly to daily basis. Up to 80% of our social and professional daily life takes place in and around cyberspace, even if we are not online. We spend on average 20–25 hours per week on the Internet, 3–4 hours a day.

Postings with a bias motive on Facebook, Instagram, or other social networks can lead to intimidation of another person, sometimes without having intended to do so. Threats, property damage, assault, murder, forced prostitution, and suicide or any other criminal offence that impairs other people's development and lives can be launched via Internet. Hate crime, such as promoting killing and murder or "shitstorms," is a type of crime that leads to physical violence that can end people's lives. It is not a specific offence. But often we do not know and neither oversee the consequences of our postings because the dynamics and dimensions of cyberspace remain unknown "territory" for us in which we cannot (yet) easily assess the consequences of our actions. It is the dimension of space and the paste by which data moves from one corner of the world to another that we have not learned to manage properly. Our current governance regimes, may it be democratic or autocratic, and our sense of justice are not (yet) adequately prepared to manage space and paste. Thus, what is "harm" in the context of cyberspace is still to be learned for many of us users. The offence derives hate speech that can lead to, for example, a person losing his or her job because there were false acclamations or private intimate images about them on Facebook which were not in line with the professional tasks the person was conducting, up to "harmless" verbal threats against a person, which were never intended to be physically executed—but eventually lead to physical harm through a third person or even suicide. The act of posting opinions, expressions, images, or comments online becomes a crime when it seriously harms others. But what "serious" harm is in cyberspace is not yet defined sufficiently.

Cybercrime is part of a cyber-war strategy and even in this context lacks common legal standards. The main difference is that war is—thus far—generally declared by a nation and its government against another nation as phrased in the UN Charta of 1945. However, that understanding of a "declared war" has changed dramatically over the past decades with expressions such as "war on drugs" first expressed in the anti-drug campaign in the USA in 1971 or "war on terror" declared by the US Bush administration in 2001 and which ever since have developed its own dynamics that eventually led to the development of the term cyber war. Cyber war takes place when a state aims to penetrate another nation's computers or networks for the purposes of causing damage or disruption. Usually, this is done through algorithm-based bots, cyber viruses, and particular programs.

Also nonstate actors, such as terrorist groups as ISIS, Hamas, and Boko Haram, use cyberspace as their platform and tool for fighting with the intention to recruit supporters and at the same time disturb and penetrate the other sides' infrastructure and weaken their institutions and regimes. Cyberwarfare is thus meant to enhance one's capability to penetrate and attack critical infrastructure on the other side (Melzer 2011). It is thus different from civil cybercrimes in a way that cybercrimes are, in general, targeted at individual people, not a state and its infrastructure. But the means, methods, and tools are the same.

Criminal and security issues are often connected to warfare and cyberwarfare and, thus, are a combination of technical warfare instruments in cyberspace. The term cyber war was already curbed in 1993 (Arquilla and Ronfeldt 1993). It thus involves the actions and intentions by a state, for example, national military or international organizations such as the NATO (CCDCOE NATO Cooperative Cyber Defence Center of Excellence 2017; Ziolkowski 2013), to attack another nation's computers or information networks through, for example, computer viruses (Maurer 2011, p. 15). Whereas "traditional" warfare always aims at a "greater objective and cause" either by claiming or defending territory or destroying political opponents who otherwise would threaten one's own nation security, cyberwarfare is about manipulating and controlling data and technical infrastructure, not territory.

In response to the dramatic rise of expenditures for cyberwarfare and cybercontrol by all countries around the world, the UN Security Council Working Group Report 2013 urges all UN member states to make careful risk assessments in cyberspace, for example, control and vigilante cyber attacks through hackers (Wolter 2013). These attacks can dramatically affect national infrastructure and destroy a whole country, for example, through ICT-enabled industrial control systems of nuclear power plants. Furthermore, if governments and other actors were to invest more in confidence-building measures in the cyber domain, for example, transparency, participation, consultation with ASEAN, AU, Arab League, OSCE, the NATO, or the EU, in adopting cybersecurity policies, this would help to regain the trust of the Internet user. Otherwise, so the concern, cybersurveillance becomes a dangerous weapon against citizens, companies, and countries without any human control (Wolter 2013). In this context, it is national security agencies or the military which harms and violates human rights in cyberspace. For example, after 9/11, anti-terror Internet surveillance measures have increased dramatically in Europe, the USA, China, Russia, Saudi Arabia, Kenya, and over 100 other countries worldwide. In India, after the 2008 terror attack in Mumbai, the government passed the Information Technology Rules in 2011 which state that "anyone who finds certain web content objectionable now has the right to have that site shut down" (Radio Netherlands Worldwide 2013). This means that governments reassume sovereignty and control over whistleblowers, leaks, and others (Lotrionte 2012). Yet, the fact that NATO has put the issue of cyber war on the agenda and is one of the main promoters of this notion of cyberwarfare shows that the debate has reached all levels of international and national affairs.

Traditionally, it is a nation-state government that declares war on another nation-state's government but even in modern times, armed conflicts with virtual or real weapons are classified as wars. They often do not even involve governmental troops or military.

Although cyberwarfare has been generally defined as a specific action and activity by a state or nonstate actor such as terror groups to penetrate another nation's computers or networks for the purposes of causing damage or disruption, governments such as in China, the USA, Israel, Saudi Arabia, or Russia have made cyberwarfare an integral part of their overall military strategy. These strategies include preemptive strikes to prevent cyber attacks against critical infrastructure, such as energy or nuclear supplies and even media propaganda. But when using war terminology, it would entail that any cyber war needs a cyber peace but among which parties will there be a "cyber peace contract" if no government or sovereign agent is officially involved and the combatants hide behind anonymous masks or social bots? Is it the battle among an army of mercenary-hackers of which many are teenagers and fully responsible for their actions or lose algorithms? Who would sign such a peace accord: the hackers? Many more of these questions lead to the same conclusion; the current hierarchical forms of governance, even in representative democracies, will not be able to respond to the demands of the new cyber world and its users as they did before. We do not need a separate digital rights agenda for this but a new type of governance based on good governance and democratic principles.

Adversary parties in war-like situations have changed dramatically over the past decades. Warlords, terror groups, or radical movements have become the frequent adversary party to declare war on each other or against governments. The phenomenon is not new but what is novel is the fact that nonstate actors can be hardly held accountable by international law in armed conflicts—less so in cyber war situations. The International Criminal Court (ICC) in The Hague with its unique universal jurisdiction in cases of war crimes and crimes against humanity has responded to the rising need to hold combatants and individuals accountable regardless of whether they are state or nonstate actors. The court claims to hold individuals accountable for war crimes and crimes against humanity regardless of their affiliation. It thus aims to fill a gap of international law under which traditionally only nations and their governments were held accountable—for example, through the UN International Court of Justice (ICJ). There has been no case in front of the ICC thus far of a cyber war-criminal, i.e., hacker or software engineer that works for ISIS or Boko Haram, but it could well be the fact in the future. If a technical engineer programmed computer virus in the name of ISIS that destroyed the whole water or sanitary infrastructure of a district or a region and therefore led to massive deaths, one could consider his or her liability under universal criminal jurisdiction, regardless of his or her citizenship. We have not seen it yet, but it would be legally possible to identify such responsibility in the context of cyber war and to hold programmers accountable in front of an international court.

Hence, the claim for a global cyber court who regulates cases not only of cybercrimes that cannot be dealt with domestically or cross-border could also be active in unsolved cases of cyber war. In 2009, the NATO's cyber defense center in Tallin, Estonia, launched the Tallin Manual with the aim of highlighting the fact that International Law during physical war is also valid during cyberwarfare and that states have to take any possible efforts to uphold these standards (CCDCOE 2013). Offline or online war requires the same standards and consequences for those who violate humanitarian or human rights law.

Acts of cybercrime seem to happen more often in countries in which democracy is weak and the rule of law absent. These countries allow for loopholes for providers and hackers to use and penetrate the Internet in a way that allows for widespread violation of human rights. Thus, it is by no surprise that governments of those countries often complain about the level of crime and violence of data and hate speech traced back to IP addresses in their countries. In Central Asia, for example, the cybercrime rate is particularly high. The governments of Kazakhstan, Tajikistan, Uzbekistan, and Kyrgyz Republic, known for their poor human rights or rule of law record, have tripled the access to the Internet among citizens over the past 10 years with subsequent consequences for the crime rates. Governmental facilities face massive cases of hooliganism, hacktivism, and cyber fraud. In 2010, a 14-year-old young man resident of Russia hacked into the National Space Agency of Kazakhstan by creating a user account with administrator rights. When traced back in Russia, the boy argued in his defense that the developers of the security program of the Space Agency did not sufficiently protect the portal and that he just wanted to show how vulnerable it was (Kutnaeva 2014, pp. 15–17). By claiming that it was the Agency's fault to not protect adequately and because cybercrimes were not sufficiently defined neither in Russia nor in Kazakhstan, the boy could avoid severe charges against him. In particular, governmental websites and services are under hacker attack in these countries, not only because they are poorly protected but also because users see for the first time an opportunity to demonstrate directly to their governments their discontent with the regimes. "Hacktivism" has become a new form of political opposition in these countries and illustrates not only discontent with the regime but also a claim for more transparency, accountability, and participation within the country.

In response to this growing number of cybercrimes, may they be petty or severe; in September 2016, the government of Malaysia has created the first special cyber court for the country in response to the data corruption via the Internet. The court is operating like any other court handling cases of corruption and anti-profiteering but is meant as a pilot to see whether it works more effectively if it is specialized on cybercrimes that due to its dimensions, consequences, and paste are different from other administrative or civil crimes (The Mailaymail Online 2016).

Governmental rhetorics about leaks in the cyberspace often include organic terms, such as cyber-attacks by virus, infections, etc., which suggests that the

Internet is "alive" and therefore requires preventive, defensive measures, similar to global diseases and threat to health. But in the case of cyber war, the "enemy" could be an algorithm and a social bot that cannot be traced back to a software engineer. At the same time, the bot is affecting millions of programs and computers in the world and does not behave according to any code of human conduct whatsoever—even in the context of martial law. Social bots are not known for their empathy or emotions. Nonetheless, state governments such as the US or British government have reacted in an often precipitant way to these threats. This has been demonstrated by the scandal around PRISM and the whistleblower Edward Snowden in 2013 and the case of WikiLeaks founder Assange. None of these cases seems to be resolved, let alone in a way that would mean more data protection, privacy, and freedom for all Internet users on a global level. The often overhasty reactions by the government concerning secret data files show the helplessness and shortcomings of the current legislative bodies and the judiciary when it comes to cybercrimes.

Interestingly enough, these scandals curbed the term "cyber espionage" when publishing confidential secret service data in the name of transparency being made public by individual agents. Software engineers and even CSOs are made responsible for "espionage" against states regardless of their intentions, instead of calling them what they are: whistleblowers—an antagonism which exemplifies the lack of definition and clarification in these aspects. These and many more cases also illustrate that the "enemy of tomorrow" is not the state army or a corrupt government but can be a single person who hacks and leaks confidential data, may it be private or national security data, and he or she makes it public without consent but with intentions of which this person may not even estimate the consequences for others.

References

Arquilla, J., & Ronfeldt, D. (1993). Cyberwar is coming! *Comparative Strategy, 12*, 141–165.

CCDCOE. (2013). *Tallinn manual*. Accessed April 19, 2017, from https://ccdcoe.org/research.html

CCDCOE NATO Cooperative Cyber Defence Center of Excellence. (2017). Accessed April 19, 2017, from https://www.ccdcoe.org/

Council of Europe. (2001). *Convention on cybercrime*. http://www.europarl.europa.eu/meetdocs/2014_2019/documents/libe/dv/7_conv_budapest_/7_conv_budapest_en.pdf

Council of Europe. (2017). *Action against cybercrime*. Accessed April 19, 2017, from https://www.coe.int/en/web/cybercrime

Eskens, S., van Daalen, O., & van Eijk, N. (2015). *Ten standards for oversight and transparency of national intelligence services*. Accessed April 19, 2017, from http://ivir.nl/publicaties/download/1591

European Court of Human Rights. (2015, June 16). *Case Delfi AS v. Estonia, No. 64569/09*.

European Court of Human Rights. (2012, December 18). *Case Yildirim v. Turkey, No. 158*.

Freedom Online Coalition. (2017). *The freedom online coalition*. Accessed April 19, 2017, from https://www.freedomonlinecoalition.com/

INSAFE-INHOPE Network. (2014). *Annual report 2014*. Accessed April 19, 2017, from http://inhope.org/Libraries/Annual_reports/Joint_Insafe_INHOPE_Annual_Report_2014.sflb.ashx

Internet Jurisdiction. (2017). Accessed April 19, 2017, from http://www.internetjurisdiction.net/

Kutnaeva, N. (2014). The fight against internet, crimes must not neglect democratic principles in concordiam. *Journal of European Security and Defense Issues, 5*(2), 15–17.

Lipton, J. (2015). *Rethinking cyberlaw: A new vision for internet law*. Cheltenham: Edward Elgar Publishing.

Lotrionte, C. (2012). State sovereignty and self-defense in cyberspace: A normative framework for balancing legal rights. *Emroy International Law Review, 26*(1), 825–919. Accessed April 19, 2017, from http://www.law.emory.edu/fileadmin/journals/eilr/26/26.2/Lotrionte.pdf.

Maurer, T. (2011). *Cyber norm emergence at the United Nations – An analysis of the UN's activities regarding cyber-security?*. Accessed April 19, 2017, from http://belfercenter.ksg.harvard.edu/files/maurer-cyber-norm-dp-2011-11-final.pdf

Melzer, N. (2011). *Cyberwarfare in international law*. Accessed April 19, 2017, from http://unidir.org/files/publications/pdfs/cyberwarfare-and-international-law-382.pdf

OSCE Office for Democratic Institutions and Human Rights. (2014). *Hate crime laws: A practical guide*. Accessed April 19, 2017, from osce.org/odihr

Radio Netherlands Worldwide. (2013). *Stricter Indian internet laws 'threaten human rights'*. Accessed April 19, 2017, from http://www.rnw.nl/english/article/stricter-indian-internet-laws-threaten-human-rights

The Mailaymail Online. (2016). *Cyber court to roll out Sept 1, Azalina tells lawyers to deepen IT knowledge*. Accessed April 19, 2017, from http://www.themalaymailonline.com/malaysia/article/cyber-court-to-roll-out-sept-1-azalina-tells-lawyers-to-deepen-it-knowledge#sthash.MkxPdSyu.dpuf

Wolter, D. (2013). *The UN takes a big step forward on cybersecurity: Arms control today*. Accessed April 19, 2017, from https://www.armscontrol.org/act/2013_09/The-UN-Takes-a-Big-Step-Forward-on-Cybersecurity

Ziolkowski, K. (Ed.). (2013). *Peacetime regime for state activities in cyberspace*. Tallinn: CCDCOE NATO Cooperative Cyber Defence Center of Excellence. Accessed January 1, 2017.

Chapter 7
Shrinking Space

E-mails, websites, social networks, and apps in general are not per se safe platforms or tools to transfer private data. But platforms and e-mails have the potential to be a safer place in cyberspace if the Internet becomes a neutral provider of data communication. That is to say, the Internet does not per se guarantee a safe haven for data and our privacy rights to be safeguarded. We can look at cyberspace not as an actor but as a virtual space which we aim to "civilize" by the means of neutral Internet. If users no longer trust its neutrality because of impairment of their data transfer, they will stop using it. By blocking, slowing down data transfer, taking down or deleting social and critical websites as well as networks, through governmental surveillance, the space shrinks. Shrinking also means laming, when the speed of the Internet slows down and as a result of it people cannot use it for quick messages or online search, as, for example, organizing and looking up meeting points for demonstrations, urgent actions, etc. Access to fast Internet speed can be costly and only available to those who have the financial means. Thus, to charge for fast Internet access also impairs the access to neutral Internet.

Due to lack of control and governance of the space and paste, many Internet users claim to be in the current state of "post privacy" in which everyone has a long trail of data that at any time potentially allows for retroactive actions by anyone at any time on a global scale. Data can be misused and abused by national security agencies and local authorities, by private providers, or by ourselves (Appelbaum 2013).

But the shrinking space of cyberspace is also determined by the limits, censorships, and even charges issued by security agencies and governments against CSOs, political activist, HRD, bloggers, or whistleblowers who use the space to participate, advertise, or campaign for their interests. For example, Amnesty International has a campaign for Raif Badawi, a Saudi Arabian blogger who is sentenced to 10 years imprisonment and 1000 lashes and 195,000 € penalty (if he survives the flogging) because he objected against the autocratic regime in his country (Amnesty International UK 2016). Apart from the questions whether Badawi raised serious criticism against the Kingdom's government or not, the question remains whether

A. Mihr, *Cyber Justice*, SpringerBriefs in Political Science,
DOI 10.1007/978-3-319-60093-2_7

these sentences against someone who used the web as a platform to express peacefully his ideas is adequate or not. Or whether the governmental response illustrates the flaws of a regime and its legal system to deal with Internet activism and the access to Internet as such.

Similar questions arise not only in autocratic regimes where the political activist always suffers consequences with or without the Internet. In the USA, for example, looking at the case of a young soldier and IT specialist Chelsea Elizabeth Manning who in 2013 was charged 35 years of prison for whistleblowing secret CIA information about the warfare in Iraq and its possible violation of international humanitarian law. She used the Internet as a platform to transmit this confidential information. Amnesty International had been urging the US government for immediate release because in Amnesty's view she did not violate any laws that would justify such a harsh sentence (Amnesty International USA 2016). Manning was early released from prison in 2017. The dramatic dimension of this act was not whether this information was primarily confidential or not—it was confidential—but the point was that by posting this information on the web and making it potentially accessible for four billion users and all governments around the world, no countermeasure or any form of damage control can delete this information from cyberspace—ever. It is this dimension concerning the medium and long-term consequences of posting confidential or private data on the web, which no one can yet really foresee. The disclosure of this kind of information as such would lead to charges in a country around the world, but the dimension of the disclosure is different if one posts this data online.

Hence, apart from legal questions about the violation of humanitarian or human rights law caused by US intelligence operation and warfare in Iraq, the question remains on what charges are justified and adequate if people post confidential or private information on the web—whatever higher or lower cause it may serve? One of the short-term consequences of the helplessness of governments to deal with this situation is to close down websites, to hunt whistleblowers, and to shrink cyberspace wherever possible.

Raif Badawi, for example, would have not received the same sentence if he would have written a letter or distributed a leaflet in front of the Kings palace as his outreach would have been smaller. However, he did get an unusual high sentence when posting his criticism in an online blog which is accessible to the whole world. The International Commission of Jurist, one of the oldest leading human rights NGOs in the world, established already in the 1950s an office in Geneva. The International Commission of Jurist has consultancy status with the UN High Commissioner for Human Rights and distributes annual lists on so-called counter-terrorism actions by governments against online human rights activism and HRD that use the Internet to promote human rights. Each year in its e-bulletin, the Commission cites hundreds of cases around the world naming bloggers in Ethiopia or Bangladesh that criticize governments or make corruption transparent, imprisonments of HRDs and journalists in Turkey that publish online, and whistleblowers in the USA and India that are in detention for exercising their human rights using the Internet as a platform for posting confidential matters (International Commission of Jurists 2017).

Counter-terrorism measures have thus often been used by governments to shut down websites and deny access to them. The dramatic growth of closures and bans of bloggers has framed and lined the idea of shrinking spaces. It has also led to establish fear and self-censorship among bloggers, many ending their activities because of threats. In line with counter-terrorism measures that are often named as an excuse to shrinking spaces, another argument brought up by governments is that of safeguarding human security. Human security is a people-centered view of security that is necessary for national, regional, and global stability. It is about securing "freedom from want" and "freedom from fear" for all persons and, therefore, to assure human rights for all as the best path to tackle the problem of global or local insecurity (Human Development Reports 1994, p. 24). Authorities who close down platforms, networks, or websites can argue that they do this in the name of security and the *Gemeinwohl*. However, often these measures happen after a terror attack or strong political outcry and are used as a proxy to shrink spaces. Behind it stands the overwhelming helplessness of governments to control and govern the cyberspace in all its rapid and seemingly endless dimensions.

Political security, instead, is an argument often used by the Internet community that aims for unlimited use of cyberspace. It is concerned with whether people live in a society that honors their fundamental freedoms. This level of security is more likely to be achieved if Internet users can participate in decision-making and legislative processes of their country according to international human rights law standards and if these laws later are complied with the so-called rule of law—which is a current claim for neutral Internet and the free use of cyberspace (T. Guedes da Costa 2008).

Altogether, cybersecurity aims to balance between the closure of the Internet on the one side and the unlimited access to it without any control whatsoever on the other side. Cybersecurity is a way to avoid shrinking spaces by means of technical tools, policies, security concepts, guidelines, risk management approaches, actions and Internet literacy programs that can be used to protect the cyber environment and users' assets at any time at any place in the endless space and at the same time avoids harm to third parties or persons by posting confidential or private data. Cybersecurity, therefore, strives to ensure the attainment and maintenance of the security properties of users' assets, data, and information against relevant security risks in the cyber environment. The general security objectives are comprised of the integrity of information, data authenticity, and nonrepudiation and aim to secure data in a confidential manner (International Telecommunication Union 2017). However, this security concept faces the challenge of allowing and even encouraging whistleblowers to shed worldwide light on illicit, illegal, and wrongful acts of companies or governments. For this to justify, we need to better understand the consequences of our action when leaking information and data.

In a critical theory of cyberspace, Michael Froomkin (2003) phrases this dilemma as, namely, the Internet is in principle a neutral tool that can be instrumentalized in various ways, promoting human rights and at the same time violating human rights, and thus, the Internet has the potential to infringe our security. The way we perceive the Internet depends on the deliberative and effective participation through us and, thus, the kind of rules, standards, and limits we set in the Internet. Consequently, this will determine the quality of political and societal systems or regimes and automatically the security (Froomkin 2003). Therefore, protecting and securing this data for the use that does not harm deliberative communication is one of the top priorities of the cybersecurity regime. Bearing in mind that the number of Internet users in 2000 was around 360 million and today is around four billion, the urgency for setting up common norms and standards for the Internet, to be used both by private and public actors and sectors, is high. Froomkin and others have long argued that due to the fact that online communication has risen dramatically over the past decades, we have not had time to reflect on the consequences this might have on us. Deliberation theories in Froomkin's point of view help to explain what may happen next, but not how and into what kind of directions. Due to the fact that people communicate in all aspects of life for professional, business, or private reasons via the Internet, they also exchange ideas and opinions and thus create data that seemed before impossible to generate in a lifetime. Further, this data is ungovernable by the existing institutions. At the same time, today, more people than ever have a common understanding of privacy, freedom, and human rights, but they express and execute them differently. The limits and benchmarks according to which these norms are held account differ between societies, age groups, and cultures. For example, the common wish to express religious ideas or political opinions without harming or insulting others or being insulted in one's own religious belief is different in secular societies than in societies in which certain religions are a state doctrine. To post a cartoon of a prophet in a journal in one part of the world might be seen as a burlesque, but in another parts of the world as blasphemy—and yet the cartoon remains online despite threats, measures, or censorships by governments on the other side of the planet. An example to counteract this virtual reality is the recently created Cyberspace Administration of China (CAC). CAC is a governmental intelligence agency that is empowered by a plethora of laws and regulations to control and surveil networks, providers, and users under a broad mandate to preserve "Internet sovereignty" as a core function of national security. The term alone illustrates the main dilemma and challenge governments face in this context, which is to gain "sovereignty" over a space that they de facto do not control in the first place. With the fastest growing user rate in the world—above 700 million—in only a few years, China's countless efforts to shrink the space seem helpless. The fact that China has created control agents for the Internet is not different from all other states who have such units, but the novelty is that the Chinese Communist Party and the President Xi Jinping is in direct control of it. Thus, there is no independent (let alone multistakeholder) agency to monitor the Internet and report abuse or human rights violation but only a small committee of party leaders and members of the Politburo to set the directives and indicators on what and how to monitor. The definition of "sovereignty" for 700 million users is entirely left in the hands of a few advisors to the Politburo (Bandurski 2015). In December 2015, in his speech about cybersecurity, president Xi made clear that cyber sovereignty is all about legitimizing cyber censorship and exporting the idea of Chinese-style cyber censorship to the rest of the world (Freeweibo 2015b). This bold statement highlights the government's open declaration to fight any free movement of data and information, but to the outside observer it looks like a fight against windmills. Instead, the Internet-based social movements, which organize themselves against the Communist Party, grow much faster than any international pressure could ever do. The Party fears a spillover from other recent "Facebook" or Internet-based revolutions to China, such as those in the Arab world, which had dramatic and violent consequences. The leadership aims at allowing free but controlled access to the Internet for everyone. They avoid close collaboration on the international level which would stop them censorship to avoid any type of political or "color revolution" in China (Freeweibo 2015a; Hansel 2013). The government invests immense amounts of human and financial resources in the securitization of the Internet in order to prevent any interference of its own citizens in the political affairs. The impact of these governmental policies might be limited, but the consequences for the society at large can yet not fully be foreseen. Despite the countries' size and massive control mechanisms, it questionable if the government alone can fully seek control over the Internet's use by its citizens.

Because there is no generally agreed social cyber contract (yet), the most common way of governmental response to the "inadequate" use of freedom on the Internet is through censorship. Governments, national security, and intelligent agencies react similarly to those who post hate speeches. It is often arbitrary and without clear limits or benchmarks on what is allowed to be exchanged on the Internet and what not. Thus, cybersecurity is not only challenged by insulting user posts that lead to mobbing and automatically harming other peoples' human rights but in similar ways through governmental intelligence agencies. Those launch algorithms and bots to infringe people's privacies, censor their websites, and penetrate their personal safety and development. In this line, Hansel (2013) phrased cybersecurity as a public and common good that needs to be protected through all, including the users themselves. Stronger democratically developed countries, which are based on the rule of law, protect the safety and security of their Internet citizens generally better than weaker and undemocratic countries. The latter often becomes safe havens for cyber criminals to commit attacks against governmental institutions, because hackers in these countries (governmental or private) do not fear any repercussions or litigations (Hansel 2013). In conclusion, the cybersecurity regime has become an abusive one because it lacks a human rights-based approach to global rules and regulations. But even though there would be such rules and regulations, the attitudes and behaviors of policy makers and judges do not change easily. For example, the notorious and dubious Law No 5651 from 2006 in Turkey allows for an almost unlimited censorship, closure of websites, and the persecution of CEOs or service providing companies, politicians, or HRD when using online platforms for their activities. The Turkish Ministry of Justice was successful in passing this law that allows for unlimited interferences in the name of cybercrime and counter-terrorism and thus undermined democratic movements in the country long before the coup in 2016 (Akdeniz and Altiparmak 2008). Awareness in raising programs and the training of judges would be a first step to make best use of the legal provisions that exist and avoid abuses.

Online spaces, which are for CSOs (often) their (only) way to express and interact with society through Internet, have been shrinking. Closing down websites is rather harmless, but tracing IP addresses and HRD via data trails to infringe civil society activities has led to serious change of behavior. The International Federation for Human Rights, one of the oldest human rights movements in the world, is raising serious concerns about "shrinking space" for civil society and users. Together with Amnesty International, Human Rights Watch, and many other international human rights organizations including the UN High Commissioner for Human Rights, the organization has warned of the underestimated consequences this may have for democratic developments but also economic growth. The Internet, once seen as a promising tool to promote human rights and democracy beyond authoritarian regimes, is under scrutiny. In Brazil, for example, the government has massively supported the national Brazilian Internet Steering Committee, a national IGF, to promote and monitor, with a 10-point agenda, human rights democratic and collaborated legal and regulatory governance (Brazilian Internet Steering Committee 2017). But at the same time, the government failed to uphold the simplest principles of the rule of law during the impeachment policies against the president in 2015 and 2016. This indicated that the democratic principles matter less when private and corporate interests are in the forefront. Many dreams and ideals are projected to the possibilities the Internet may bring, but it is easily forgotten that if governments do not respect the rule of law or human rights norms offline, they will not care much about them online as well. Thus, the UN organizations and the CSO movement claim that "in many countries the authorities place considerable restrictions on civil society's free space by not hesitating to overstep the law with the support of the judiciary or by adopting laws which increasingly threaten freedom and which focus particularly on NGOs' and CSOs' access to funding, registration requirements, and controlling the activities of organizations or freedom of assembly" (FIDH World Wide Movement for Human Rights 2017).[1] But as earlier indicated, these constraints and closures might not last for long due to the setup of the cyberspace. Despite increasing governmental laws and bills "regulating" the activities of CSOs and to restrict access to public or international funding, particularly when sourced from abroad, CSOs continue to exist—although often less web-based then before—in countries such as China, Russia, Nigeria, or Turkey. But their range of action without free movement in cyberspace is limited. Reversed tendencies to shrinking space are also seen in the role of "matured" and independent court decision in favor of freedom on the Internet. In March 2015, the Supreme Court of India has struck down Section 66A of the Information Technology Act that was proclaimed in 2013. Prior to the act, the number of whistleblowers in India rose, making corruption and misconduct of local authorities public via the Internet.

[1]See more at: FIDH World Wide Human Rights Movement (2017). https://www.fidh.org/en/issues/human-rights-defenders/shrinking-space-for-civil-society/. Accessed 19 April 2017; and UN High Commissioner for Human Rights (2016). Hate is Being Mainstreamed – Global Update by the High Commissioner, June 2016. http://www.ohchr.org/EN/NewsEvents/Pages/GlobalhumanrightsupdatebyHC.aspx#sthash.eUJkYvhH.dpuf. Accessed 19 April 2017.

So it happened to the chief engineer of the Water Resource Department in a state in India, Vijay Pandhare, in 2012, who was sentenced to several years in prison for leaking sensitive data about corruption in the department (Landau 2013; Pallavi 2012). The whistleblower claimed to have made public the misconduct of a publicly run company (Deibert and Crete-Nishihata 2012). Since 2013, the act had led to massive closure of a website and thus to shrinking space. In the legal order, the court said, Section 66A is violative of the freedom of expression and speech rights enshrined in the constitution of India, which is as such a pillar of democracy in the country. In its argumentation, the judges stated that there is a difference between discussion, advocacy, and incitement. Discussion and advocacy in favor or against political decisions and policies, no matter how annoying they might be, is allowed. It is part of the liberty and liberty of thought in the country. The threshold, however, would be when web-based discussions become harmful for other persons. The former Information and Broadcasting Minister of India welcomed the judgment. He said that Section 66A was misused too often in the context of combating terrorism and national security and instead weakened the democracy in the country and hence it needed to go. And Rinu Srinivasan, one of the girls who was arrested under this section for a Facebook post criticizing governmental policies, said, "(...) if this law is repealed it may encourage people to speak up and against all the wrong in the world. (. . .) I am very happy. I feel like we have received justice after two years" (Radio Netherlands Worldwide 2013).

But the phenomena to control or shrink the use of cyberspace are not new. The novelty is that this space has been penetrated by governmental agencies dramatically over the past years. In 2013, according to the Freedom in the Net Index, half of the indexed countries (that have high rate of access to the Internet in their territory) censor Internet freedom. State security agencies, Internet police or hackers-for-hire, use different methods to disturb, filter, or censor the exercise of freedom rights of the users. The Index cites that at least in 29 out of 60 states, blocking and filtering of information and platforms in the Internet is a common practice (Kelly et al. 2013). Cyberattacks that take place on dissidents and human rights advocates or paid pro-government bloggers, for example, in China, Bahrain, or in Russia, are a daily annoyance. And by 2015, this number was rising. Official numbers count that 42 out of the 65 states use Internet surveillance technology to penetrate users activities. The unknown figures are likely to be much higher. The Freedom Index Report (2016) states that governments censor information of public interest while also expanding surveillance and cracking down on privacy tools. Governments and their intelligence remove content from private and CSOs' websites (Freedom House 2016). They urge private companies or Internet users to restrict and delete web content dealing with political, religious, or social and political issues in the name of state security. Bloggers get intimidated and imprisoned for sharing information concerning politics, religion, or the overall society through digital networks. The number of surveillance laws and technologies multiplied. In 2015 alone, 14 out of 65 countries' governments passed new laws to increase surveillance (Kelly et al. 2015). Democracies and authoritarian regimes alike stigmatized encryption as an instrument of terrorism, and many tried to ban or limit tools that protect privacy

(Kelly et al. 2015). If people claim their privacy, it also means that governmental security agencies have less access to their data or have to justify the breach of it. Thus, protecting privacy rights in cyberspace can also lead to conflicts with governments that claim to uphold state security in the fight against terror. Access to our bank accounts or insurance companies, our flight, and travel bookings are a breach of private data but can be accessed by governments without restrictions if the laws allow to do so.

But the threat to freedom and dignity on the Internet does not only come from governments and hackers, but from users and private media companies who post false defamatory information and hate speech that shrinks the space of the addressee. Cyber mobbing or cyber bulling occurs when a person uses Internet tools to embarrass, threaten, harass, or otherwise cause harm to individuals. It is an aggressive and intentional act of using, for example, social media, YouTube, or commentary lines to attack other people.[2] Because of its intention, these postings are harmful acts and, thus, also qualify as cybercrime. Privately or governmental launched trolls and social bots penetrate our communication and information and change our behavior in cyberspace. We become more careful about what we post and if in doubt, do not believe the information provided through social media or make no use of it at all. It is our choice, but this growing mistrust can also mislead us in not using valuable and rightful information on the Internet. Internet illiteracy and self-censorship is one of the most serious threats to Internet freedom after all. Although, social bots and trolls can be helpful servants to trigger debates online, they are difficult to trace back to their "creator" that is the programmer, who could be held responsible. For some social movements, in particular in the Global South, social media is the only tool to spread their messages. If this tool is infringed and penetrated, their communication tools become scare. Their voice would not be heard and the number of supporters is unlikely to grow.

Generally speaking, users start to distrust Internet services and no longer use social networks to express their ideas or to use search engines to search for certain keywords that may trigger the attention of national security agencies because of the data trail each search entry leaves behind in the World Wide Web. Users censor themselves in the way that they adapt to restrictive rules. This adaptive self-imposed censorship is not to be put on the same level as the "do no harm" rule. Self-censorship is the fear of uncontrolled repercussions after expressing a view or opinion or looking up a keyword in a search engine. In this case, the Internet becomes a political and manipulative tool that hits back to the user due to the fact that it can technically provide data on people's ideas to national security agencies or technical companies (Dahl 2015). The dynamics of social media are thus twofold and have to be seen as any information and communication tool that can serve a good and a bad cause.

---

[2]For cyber-mobbing, see University of Hannover Institute for Information Systems Research (2017). Cyber- Mobbing. http://www.archiv.iwi.uni-hannover.de/cms/images/stories/upload/lv/sosem11/Bilder/Nguyen/Website/cyber-mobbing.html. Accessed 19 April 2017.

The former president of Germany, Joachim Gauck, raised his concerns about shrinking cyberspace during his annual address to the nation in 2013. Here, he highlighted that all forms of privacy which our forefathers once used to fight for against the state and which in totalitarian regimes helped us to shield ourselves from being coerced are fading away.

> Rather than posing a threat, publicity now seems to offer the hope of appreciation and recognition. Many do not realize or simply do not want to know that they are complicit in the creation of the virtual twin to their real life self—their alter ego who reveals, or could reveal, both their strengths and weaknesses, who could disclose their failures or deficiencies, or who could even divulge sensitive information about illnesses. Who makes the individual more transparent, readily analyzed and easily manipulated by agencies, politics, commerce, and the labor market (Federal President Joachim Gauck 2013).

International governmental frameworks and agreements seek to answer these dilemma, for example, the "IP Protection Act" Preventing Real Online Threats to Economic Creativity and Theft of Intellectual Property Act (PIPA) in 2008 or the "Stop Online Privacy Act" (SOPA) in 2011 as well as during the 2012 attempt to set up an intergovernmental "Anti-Counterfeiting Trade Agreement" (ACTA) on a global level. Although the violation of copyrights and intellectual property was in the center of these agreements, they also aim to protect private data as exclusively private rights. These infringements had the potential to restrict freedom of expression, for example, scientific knowledge on medicine, technologies, art, or literature by others than the holder or author of the copyright (Wesselingh 2013). Most of these agreements had no significant consequences for the users because it became evident that a few governments alone cannot solve the problem of data protection on a global let alone cyber level. If not all governments agree and join the multi-stakeholder approach that includes actors from the nonformal and private sector such as technical corporations, search engines, Internet users, civil organizations, and so on, the agreements might not be worth more than the paper they are written on. Therefore in 2011, the CoE in Strasbourg expressed its concerns when highlighting that any Internet governance arrangements must ensure the protection of all fundamental rights and freedoms and affirm their universality, interdependence, and interrelations in accordance with international human rights law. They must also ensure full respect for democracy and the rule of law and should promote sustainable development (Declaration by the Committee of Ministers on Internet governance principles 2011; Kleinwächter 2012). Therefore, in recent international meetings, we find a mix of actors and stakeholders involved in international, regional, or national, for example, IGOs, states, CSOs, technical actors that represent providers, communication services, or search engines such as Microsoft, Apple, Google, Firefox, Yahoo, Xando, Weibo, Skype, Clouds, Dropbox, etc. or other private business actors such as online business and companies, start-ups, different App providers, Amazon, DHL, or network actors like Mxit, Wretch, Facebook, Nexopia, Google+, Badoo, XING, Hi5, Orkut, Renren, LinkedIn, Skype, and so on. The list could be continued. Implicitly, users are involved in all these categories and can have multiple functions, for example, when being a user of Renren, a customer of DHL, and working for IBM.

Internet control is an array of measures that can also lead to technical blocking (IP and URL blocking); removing search results; the take-down by regulators often according to national law, for example, in 2011 in Egypt during the revolts and in 2009 in Iran during student protests; or through self-censorship based on fear and threats of legal actions, group pressure, or intimidation by governments (OpenNet Initative 2017). Another example of a regional intergovernmental regime that aims to restrict Internet freedom is the SCO. In 2017, the Asian member states of SCO and Russia launched the coordinates policy and protective integration against democracy, regime change, and human rights in cyberspace (Shanghai Cooperation Organization 2017). Consequently, the trust and confidence in state authorities of Internet users living and working in these countries is most likely to decrease. The legitimacy and authority of institutions, organizations, companies, agencies, and practices in cyberspace might decrease (Hornsby; Peppard and Rylander 2005). Frequent and widespread national data surveillance programs jeopardize civic trust and confidence in the Internet (Wolter 2013). They are conducted by national security agencies, secret services, or private companies. Governments and national authorities using national intelligence or spyware viruses, or private corporations using business intelligence, can modify cookies on private computers to deduct data for their own purposes, for example, this happens when we leave data trails via Skype and Facebook, after online shopping, when chatting with friends and colleagues, and when using WhatsApp or Uber. We leave data trails when applying for new IDs online, using credit cards, and so on. The amount of data is massive; hardly anyone has an oversight over it, and therefore the abuse and misuse of these data is so alarming. We are no longer the owner of our own private data, and that is what leads to misconducts in cyberspace (Electronic Frontier Foundation 2013).

References

Akdeniz, Y., & Altiparmak, K. (2008). *Internet: Restricted access: A critical assessment of internet content regulation and censorship in Turkey*. Accessed April 19, 2017, from http://www.cyber-rights.org/reports/internet_restricted_bw.pdf

Amnesty International UK. (2016). *Raif Badawi*. Accessed April 19, 2017, from https://www.amnesty.org.uk/issues/Raif-Badawi

Amnesty International USA. (2016). *Chelsea manning punishment for suicide attempt is cruel and inhumane*. Accessed April 19, 2017, from http://www.amnestyusa.org/news/press-releases/chelsea-manning-punishment-for-suicide-attempt-is-cruel-and-inhumane

Appelbaum, J. (2013). *Elevate open everything*. Accessed April 19, 2017, from http://2013.elevate.at/festival/ueber-das-festival/newsmagazin/detail/news/jacob-appelbaum-elevate-open-everything/

Bandurski, D. (2015). *Re-defining cyberspace*. Accessed April 19, 2017, from http://cmp.hku.hk/2015/10/08/39309/

Brazilian Internet Steering Committee. (2017). Accessed April 19, 2017, from http://cgi.br

Council of Europe. (2011, September 21). *Declaration by the Committee of Ministers on Internet Governance Principles*.

da Costa, T. G. (2008). Political security, an uncertain concept with expanding concerns. In H. G. Brauch (Ed.), *Globalization and environmental challenges. Reconceptualizing security in the 21st century* (p. 562). Berlin: Springer.

Dahl, S. (2015). *Social media marketing: Theories and applications*. London: SAGE.

Deibert, R. J., & Crete-Nishihata, M. (2012). Global governance and the spread of cyberspace controls. *Global Governance, 18*(3). Accessed April 19, 2017, from https://www.questia.com/library/journal/1G1-301181778/global-governance-and-the-spread-of-cyberspace-controls

Electronic Frontier Foundation. (2013). *Internet surveillance and free speech: The United Nations Makes the connection*. Accessed April 19, 2017, from https://www.eff.org/deeplinks/2013/06/internet-and-surveillance-UN-makes-the-connection

Federal President Joachim Gauck. (2013). *Speech by Federal President Joachim Gauck to mark the day of German unity*. Accessed April 19, 2017, from http://www.bundespraesident.de/SharedDocs/Downloads/DE/Reden/2013/10/131003-Tag-Deutsche-Einheit-englische-Uebersetzung.pdf?__blob=publicationFile

FIDH World Wide Movement for Human Rights. (2017). Accessed April 19, 2017, from https://www.fidh.org/en/issues/human-rights-defenders/shrinking-space-for-civil-society/

Freedom House. (2016). *Freedom in the world*. Accessed April 19, 2017, from https://freedomhouse.org/report/freedom-world/freedom-world-2016

Freeweibo. (2015a, December 16). Accessed April 19, 2017, from https://freeweibo.com/

Freeweibo. (2015b, December 19). Accessed April 19, 2017, from https://freeweibo.com/

Froomkin, A. M. (2003). Habermas@discourse.net: Toward a critical theory of cyberspace. *Harvard Law Review, 116*(3), 749–873.

Hansel, M. (2013). *Cyber security governance and the theory of public goods*. Accessed April 19, 2017, from http://www.e-ir.info/2013/06/27/cyber-security-governance-and-the-theory-of-public-goods/

Hornsby, W. E. The ethical boundaries of selling legal services in cyberspace. *National Law Journal*. Accessed April 19, 2017, from http://www.kuesterlaw.com/netethics/abawill.htm

Human Development Reports. (1994). *Chapter 2: New dimension of human security*. Accessed April 19, 2017, from http://hdr.undp.org/en/reports/global/hdr1994/chapters/

International Commission of Jurists. (2017). Accessed April 19, 2017, from https://www.icj.org/

International Telecommunication Union. (2017). *Definition of cybersecurity*. Accessed April 19, 2017, from http://www.itu.int/en/ITU-T/studygroups/com17/Pages/cybersecurity.aspx

Kelly, S., Earp, M., Reed, L., Shabaz, A., & Truong, M. (2015). *Freedom on the net 2015: Privatizing censorship, eroding privacy*. Accessed April 19, 2017, from https://freedomhouse.org/sites/default/files/FOTN%202015%20Full%20Report.pdf

Kelly, S., Truong, M., Earp, M., Reed, L., Shahbaz, A., & Greco-Stoner, A. (2013). *Freedom on the net 2013: A global assessment of internet and digital media*. Accessed April 19, 2017, from http://freedomhouse.org/sites/default/files/resources/FOTN%202013_Full%20Report_0.pdf

Kleinwächter, W. (Ed.). (2012). *Human rights and internet governance*. Co:llaboratory Discussion Paper Series No. 1. Berlin, Baku.

Landau, S. (2013). Making sense from Snowden: What's significant in the NSA surveillance revelations. *IEE Computer and Reliability Societies*, 54–63. Accessed April 19, 2017, from https://www.computer.org/cms/Computer.org/ComputingNow/pdfs/MakingSenseFromSnowden-IEEESecurityAndPrivacy.pdf

OpenNet Initative. (2017). Accessed April 19, 2017, from https://opennet.net/

Pallavi, A. (2012). *Reservoir of corruption*. Accessed April 19, 2017, from http://www.downtoearth.org.in/content/reservoir-corruption

Peppard, J., & Rylander, A. (2005). Products and service in cyberspace. *International Journal of Information Management, 25*(4), 335–345. Accessed April 19, 2017, from https://dspace.lib.cranfield.ac.uk/bitstream/1826/2687/1/Products%20and%20Services%20in%20cyberspace%20-%202005.pdf.

Radio Netherlands Worldwide. (2013). *Stricter Indian internet laws 'threaten human rights'*. Accessed April 19, 2017, from http://www.rnw.nl/english/article/stricter-indian-internet-laws-threaten-human-rights

Shanghai Cooperation Organization. (2017). Accessed April 21, 2017, from http://www.sectsco.org/EN123

Wesselingh, E. (2013). *The magic show of balancing the enforcement of copyright and freedom of expression*. Proceedings of the International Conference on ICT Law 2013.

Wolter, D. (2013). *The UN takes a big step forward on cybersecurity: Arms control today*. Arms Control Association. Accessed January 1, 2017, from https://www.armscontrol.org/act/2013_09/The-UN-Takes-a-Big-Step-Forward-on-Cybersecurity

Chapter 8
Code of Conduct

In 1996, John Perry Barlow published the first of many efforts to seek a new type of social contract for the cyberspace, the "Declaration of Independence of Cyberspace." In this declaration, he indicated the situations and controversies that today's Internet users experience on a day-to-day basis (Barlow 1996). The declaration sets out in 16 short paragraphs, a rebuttal to governance of the Internet by any outside force, specifically state governments. He argues that no government had at that time the consent of the Internet users to apply arbitrary laws, censorships, and restrictions to the World Wide Web. If governments would nevertheless agree to do so, Barlow argues, as with the data protection and surveillance laws, information and data will continue to be published through whistleblowers, hackers, and "leakers" without the owner's consent. In other words, the anarchy in cyberspace will not allow for the commonly known mode of governance because the Internet requires a different form of governance than we are familiar with in the offline world. In his prognosis, Barlow assures that the Internet community and, thus, the global user community has to develop its own social contracts to determine how to handle its problems based on the golden rule, which is the basis of any human right and the "do-no-harm rule." The rule can be interpreted in such a way that if a user does not want to have his or her own private data, pictures, letters, images, or intellectual property and ideas to be publically disposed or leaked without one's prior consent, then one should also not dare to publish someone else's data without that person's consent. Of course, reality, even cyber reality, is far away from that practice, but it is an ideal benchmark against which users' behavior can be assessed. Whether such a social contract for the cyberspace will ever be realized or not remains open. But the idea is that if there ever will be a cyber or Internet governance regime, individual responsibility and adherence to human rights will be one of the guiding principles to govern that space.

Another protagonist who put forward a code of conduct for the Internet is Jeff Jarvis. He manifests that every citizen of this world needs to enjoy the right to connect and access to the Internet in order to speak freely, assemble, and enjoy his or her privacy. Eventually, this can only be guaranteed with free and neutral access

A. Mihr, *Cyber Justice*, SpringerBriefs in Political Science,
DOI 10.1007/978-3-319-60093-2_8

to public information and spheres through Internet (Jarvis 2010). But in order to maintain freedom and neutrality, everyone has to use the web according to common rules and standards.

The early years of cyberspace were the times of big ideas and visions, and, thus, the sociologist Amitai Etzioni (1999) argued that the dispute about how we define and execute privacy in cyberspace will become an indicator for how we want to be governed in the future in light of the growing Internet and cyber world. At the same time, when Internet pioneers such as Barrow and Jarvis raised their concerns, knowing at that time that the Internet would become a mass tool and mobile phones would introduce the World Wide Web to billions of people in parts of the world where traditional IT communication tools let alone democratic forms of governance had been absent, Etzioni argued that good societies ought to balance individual rights and social responsibilities, autonomy and the common good, privacy, and concerns for public safety and public health, for example. Rather than allow one value or principle (such as freedom of expression) to dominate other principles (such as privacy), we need to balance and negotiate the consensus. He goes on and highlights that for a good public policy culture, we ought to accept the concept of balance as a guiding principle. But the question arises as to how we are to determine whether our Internet policy and, thus, our code of conduct and laws are off balance and in what direction they need to move and to what extent if we want to restore balance (Etzioni 1999).

The good news is that since the UN resolution (68/167) in 2013, basic human rights principles are no longer disputed to be valid only offline but also online. Principles, such as solidarity, freedom, and justice, are universal and ingrained in any human rights treaty. However, the way governments implement and enforce or not these principles and international treaty law is yet different from country to country. There is vast agreement that freedom, justice, privacy, and security are important. However, among the four billion Internet users, not everyone will have the same ideas about their realization and implementation of human rights. The balance that Etzioni is arguing for would thus best be manifested through the principle of a code of conduct and a global social contract. Thus, there is the claim that according to these general freedom principles and norms, a social contract for cyberspace could be established. This contract would need to be enforced by all Internet users, regardless whether they are private or public, companies or governments, and so on. Rolf and Romana Weber (2008) paraphrase that the heterogeneity of Internet users originating from different geographical zones, linguistic areas, and cultural backgrounds lead to very different conceptions of norms and standards related to the organization of the Internet. But any decision about how to govern the cyberspace needs to be supported by a large part of the Internet community in order to ensure its effective functioning. Thus, transparency and participation is fundamental in this context. A multistakeholder approach enhances the information flows between the individual users, CSOs (civil society network), governments, and providers that allow the public to form an opinion and participate in negotiations. But consensus building, which includes all interested parties and creates the opportunity to make decisions, is more pivotal in the cyberspace than ever before in any offline world, as Weber argues (Weber and Weber 2008).

First steps in this direction were also launched by the EU. On the 31 May of 2016 in Brussels, the EU Commission presented together with Facebook, Microsoft, Twitter, and YouTube a "Code of conduct on countering illegal hate speech online." The main purpose was to have in place clear and effective processes to review notifications regarding illegal hate speech on their services so they can remove or disable access to such content, to motivate other companies to agree on the common rules clarifying that they prohibit the promotion of incitement to violence and hateful conduct (European Commission 2016).

A code of conduct is the basis for a social contract and subsequently a concept of cyber justice. It guides and enhances individual responsibility and behavior at the same time. Apart from global mechanisms that are needed to monitor and enforce it, it would include personal disguise and sanctions against those who violate human rights norms. In this vein, the claim for a "digital rights"-based social contract claims to allow the free and neutral access and use of ICTs, such as computers and digital media, for example, to information, to work, to communication, to health, to participation, to expression, to development, to assemble, etc. (United Nations Human Rights Office of the High Commissioner 2013).[1] Part of these codes is to be found in the context of the 2015 proclaimed UN Sustainable Development Goals (SDGs). Whereas personal and societal development is largely achieved through free and neutral access to the Internet and a human rights-based conduct. In the so-called Global South, at least two billion people have access to the Internet, mostly through mobile devices. These figures are 40-times higher than 10 years ago and show the rapid—however, uncontrolled and unregulated—access to the Internet. These new cyber citizens have little or no experience with democracy or rule of law and lack fundamental access to it. At the same time, the UN also promotes the multistakeholder approach, knowing that there is no other way to reach the goals by 2030. The UN highlights the conduct and that we all need to "enhance the Global Partnership for Sustainable Development, complemented by multistakeholder partnership that mobilizes and share knowledge, expertise, technology—in particular communication technology—and financial resources, to support the achievement of the SDG in all countries but in particular the developing countries" (UN General Assembly 2015). In short, there will be no realization without equal partnership and no development without a human rights-based use of the Internet. Jeffrey Sachs (2015), adviser to the UN, highlights the fact that without the Internet, none of these goals would ever come close to reality, in particular in the health, education, or food sector. If the world wants to fight poverty, it needs tools. Such a tool is the Internet and as he phrased it, the responsible use of big data, used wisely and managed to benefit all. The "wise" use of data depends also on how bots will be

---

[1]For the definition of digital rights, see: Business and Human Rights Resource Center (2017). Ranking digital rights project. https://business-humanrights.org/en/documents/ranking-digital-rights-project. Accessed 19 April 2017.

programmed, algorithms used, data generated, and made available for the well-being of all. Big data cannot only transfer knowledge to remote parts of the world but also assess, for example, massive data on climate, migration, business, epidemics, agriculture, and so on in order to launch rapid help or investments for developments (Sachs 2015).

One of the first serious international attempts to push for a digital rights treaty was on 10 December 2013, the International Human Rights day. On the occasion of the 65th anniversary of the UDHR, over 500 writers and Noble Prize winners from over 81 countries signed an open petition urging the UN to draft an international bill on digital rights. They argued that the dramatic increase of spyware on private data is undermining democracy online and offline and makes human rights null and void, and privacy an illusion, so they feared (The Guardian 2013). Reactions to their open call were internationally perceived and the petition came at a time during which different UN bodies are working on better digital rights protection. The massive international support to call for more legal binding international treaties had impact on the progress of global protection mechanism and an international binding document. But a charter or a convention on digital rights was not issued by the UN and neither by the other big player in the international arena, the EU. The EU had already established some case law on digital rights and sought no need to pursue an additional treaty body to manifest the importance that human rights would have online. Three years after this first attempt, and again around the 10 December, in 2016, over 100 policy makers, writers, CSOs, and philosophers from Germany launched another attempt for a Charter for Digital Fundamental Rights in the EU—to start with. Among them, Internet entrepreneurs such as the co-founder of Wikileaks, Daniel Domscheit-Berg, the philosopher Jürgen Habermas, and the President of the EU Parliament, Martin Schulz. The symbolic day of the launch of the claim for the Charter underlined the role human rights ought to play if an international code of conduct, a treaty, or charter for the Internet would ever come about. This time the undersigned asked for concrete steps to uphold dignity, data protection, equality, security, and freedom rights through an enhanced rule of law in the Internet. But the novelty in their claim has been the direct emphasis on the role that algorithms (Art.7) will play in our society in the future and that there needs to be control over them. The promoters of the Charter asked that every agency, governmental or private, when using automatic algorithm to penetrate the communication and information exchange with users, for example, in social media, during election campaigns or for security checks and social profiling, has to make the criteria and, thus, the essence of the algorithm transparent for each user of that particular media service, for example, Facebook or news agencies, Tinder, Amazon, Twitter, or E-mail or any other online service to which it may apply.[2] In short: the key intention of any code of conduct is to claim back human control and responsibility over the use of our data that has

[2]For more information see: BETA (2017). Wir fordern digitale Grundrechte. www.digitalcharta.eu. Accessed 19 April 2017.

become out of control and in the hands of technical engineers, artificial intelligence, and algorithms—and sometimes in the hands of hackers.

References

Barlow, J. P. (1996). *A declaration of the independence of cyberspace*. Accessed April 19, 2017, from https://www.eff.org/cyberspace-independence

Etzioni, A. (1999). *The limits of privacy*. New York: Basic Books.

European Commission. (2016, December). *Code of Conduct on countering illegal hate speech online: First results on implementation*. Directorate-General for Justice and Consumers, Fact Sheet.

Jarvis, J. (2010). *A bill of rights in cyberspace*. Accessed April 19, 2017, from http://buzzmachine.com/2010/03/27/a-bill-of-rights-in-cyberspace/

Sachs, J. D. (2015). *Data for development*. Accessed April 19, 2017, from https://www.project-syndicate.org/commentary/sustainable-development-data-by-jeffrey-d-sachs-2015-05

The Guardian. (2013). *International bill of digital rights: Call from 500 writers around the world*. Accessed April 19, 2017, from http://www.theguardian.com/world/2013/dec/10/international-bill-digital-rights-petition-text

UN General Assembly. (2015, October 21). *Transforming our world: The 2030 agenda for sustainable development*.

United Nations Human Rights Office of the High Commissioner. (2013). *Human rights indicators: A guide to measurement and implementation*. Accessed April 19, 2017, from https://unp.un.org/Details.aspx?pid=23745

Weber, R. H., & Weber, R. (2008). *Social contract for the internet community? Historical and philosophical theories for inclusion of the civil society*. GigaNet: Global internet governance academic network, annual symposium 2008. Accessed January 1, 2017, from https://papers.ssrn.com/sol3/papers.cfm?abstract_id=2798970

Chapter 9
Regulation and Control

More regulation and human control in cyberspace is one of many claims to manage, regulate, or organize the cyberspace and the Internet. But how to govern a space with half the world's population of which the majority is of minor of age and a large part of these users not even being at an age where they can be held accountable for full criminal responsibility as the Central Asian court cases have illustrated earlier? The majority does not live and enter the Internet in the Global North but in the Global South, the Internet is often accessed in regions and countries with poor human rights records and weak rule of law regimes. They face high levels of corruption, and independent cybercontrol or data protection mechanisms are not anywhere near. Yet, these regions have the highest increase in new "cyber citizens."

Since the UN General Assembly in 2013 confirmed that human rights are the key benchmarks for regulating the online world in the same way as they do the offline world, little or no progress has been made in realizing the promotion and protection of human rights in cyberspace. One reason for it is that due to above-mentioned regional developments, most cyber citizens live in countries in which governments have little or no interest in upholding human rights, their voices are hardly heard at the IGF, and their civil society is under constant pressure. Albeit Sub-Saharan African countries like Kenya, Nigeria, and South Africa have become core voices for the African continent when pushing for more protection of data flow and users rights. In Asia, most cases of breach of data are handled domestically and except for China and Indonesia, most countries are rather poorly represented on global events on the topic of Internet governance. It is mostly in these countries in which fake news, bots, and algorithms have been violating privacy and freedom rights. They remain a daily annoyance and can be little or not controlled by the institutions. Thus, progress will remain slow. The fact that most users are in the Global South, with poor protection mechanism but with a number of potential online consumers and data providers, makes them an interesting prey for e-commerce companies to win them as customers. African population, for example, makes 16.6% of the total world population, but with a third (27.7%) of Internet penetration, and thus is one of the fastest growing regions in terms of access to the Internet via mobile phones.

A. Mihr, *Cyber Justice*, SpringerBriefs in Political Science,
DOI 10.1007/978-3-319-60093-2_9

However, the continent mostly suffers under corrupt leadership and a lack of rule of law when holding service providers and telecommunication companies accountable for the breach of users' data.[1]

In its 2016 annual report, the Global Internet Society states that the breach of data, private and public, has increased to a new peak and mostly in countries outside Europe with no protection mechanisms. Mistrust of users toward services providers on the Internet is the consequence, whether these are online-shopping portals or media channels. Since once the Internet was seen as a source of truth and facts, it turns toward the opposite extreme. To win back the trust of the growing number of potential customers is today the core issue of governments, broadcasting and media companies, and private enterprises. At the same time, the Internet economy, the fastest and largest job provider in the world, will no longer grow, if trust of the customers, the users, will fail. Thus, not only the SDGs but also the world economy depends largely on the trust Internet users have in using Internet services. And in return, these users have to be better informed and engaged in the processes on what happens to their data to win back the trust that is gone. Gaining that trust will also depend on how good governance principles and human rights norms are upheld by companies and governments alike.

Any modern economy cannot allow for its citizens to lose trust and to stop online banking, online bookings, or online shopping, but also public services such as taxation, health, or education depend on online participation of citizens. If billions of users would restrict their usage of the Internet within 1 year or so, public infrastructure, particularly in Europe and North America, would collapse because many public services are only accessible online. That is why cybersecurity and data protection is part of the Internet governance regime today. Thus, because of the decreasing trust in service providers, the Internet Society has anticipated that the likeliness that we face a first "cyber-economy recession" is rather high (Internet Society 2016, pp. 16–21). Cyber attacks will increase; fraud and breach of data, mostly for financial reasons, will continue if regulatory and control mechanisms are not installed. Users' identities in the Internet, such as profiles, passwords, e-mail addresses, etc., are stolen for profit, and companies whose legal business is to use entrusted data spend more resources than ever in fighting this abuse. Thus, service providers are taking regulation in their own hands because a global Internet governance, who ought to do it, does not exist or will take time to be installed, while users lose trust every day. The e-commerce is losing money and time which they could invest in their business otherwise. At least 40 million customers' credit cards numbers have been reported stolen in 2016 (Identity Force 2017). Private and intimate data of 37 million users were reported to be published online without their consent; most of these reports came from the USA, where misuse is most often reported. The real figures are estimated way over a billion users being affected by breaches of their private data.

---

[1]See Internet World Stats 2017 http://www.internetworldstats.com/stats1.htm (Accessed 21 April 2017).

Due to the absence of a global cyber or Internet governance regime, the Internet Society has proposed a self-regulating regime calling it user-centric "security circle" through economic incentives. The circle encourages Internet users and organizations to assess jointly on the costs of the data breaches, increase transparency through data breach notification and disclosure, provide better tolls against violation of data, and the same organizations (providers and other services and companies) must be held accountable in the country they are based or where their services are accessible—which is basically everywhere. And last, they ask for an increase of incentives to invest in security by catalyzing a market for trusted and independent assessment of data security measures (Internet Society 2016, p. 21).

In light of the proposed shifts by the Internet Society, different stakeholders, actors, and agencies, such as representatives of search engines, communication platforms, or social networks, to name but a few Google, Skype, Microsoft Bing, Facebook, Twitter, Yahoo, Linkedin, Sina Weibo, Renren, Yandex, or Yamli, have grouped themselves in different forums and networks. Their services and the Internet economy have one thing in common: they are technically capable to allocate and collect large amount of data from each user, store it, and later sell it or provide it for external users. They do not only sell data to private companies but also to national security agencies. Data is a currency with flexible use.

Although in Europe and North America alone, 80% of all households use the Internet on a daily basis, at the same time an increasing number of users, namely, up to 30% of them, avoid using the Internet to express controversial opinions to avoid "shitstorms" or hate speech or to do large financial transaction because of the breach of data. And with the "Internet of Things" emerging to become part of our daily lives, the "safety guarantee" of our data will become more pivotal to ordinary consumers than ever. Instead, as illustrated earlier, the tendency of self-censorship is growing and one way to regain the trust is through regulation and rule of law (Internet Society 2016, p. 50).

The multistakeholder approach aims to respond to these developments by including governments, international organizations, such as the EU and the UN itself, as well as companies and private actors to discuss solutions. They come together via informal and formal forums and build partnerships for consultation. The IGF has been mandated by the UN and by the World Summit on the Information Society (WSIS) back in 2005 and has today over 170 representatives of UN member states. Almost all member states have been convening this forum for a multistakeholder policy dialogue (Internet Governance Forum 2016). IGFs exist also on the domestic national level and are usually hosted by Ministries and, thus, belong to the public policy arena of each of the UN member states. Participation is nevertheless voluntarily. During their annual international and domestic meetings, they attain to develop a shared understanding about the protection of data in cyberspace but they nevertheless play different roles and have different purposes and aims in these forums and networks. Governments, nevertheless, are still the sole and main decision makers, but not the only ones that take the responsibility in this new regime. Others, like the consultants from private companies and NGOs, serve as advisors and experts in these forums. Their partnerships are voluntary, with participation driven by the perceived benefits they may see emerging from the process (Mihr 2016).

The existing global public policy concept might be a way out of the dead-look of the multistakeholder approach versus a governmental run international cyber governance regime. The IGF puts cyber public policy annually on its agenda. It highlights the importance of finding a solution and a way to regulate and govern cyberspace beyond nation states, because a growing number of migrants, refugees, minors, enterprises, and governments alike have the same access to the Internet but do not follow the same rules let alone responsibilities—and thus the majority of Internet users today cannot even be held accountable for potential wrongdoings because of their uncertain status, lack of citizenship, shortage of global rules and laws.

The legal and political framework of the cyber regime is thus far enshrined in international human rights law, customary international law, trade law, and international public law—but they all have in common that they are state based and states, not Internet users, are the main reference point. In times of over 100 million uprooted people worldwide, of which most are using the Internet as their tool to survive and live, the current international legal frameworks seems insufficient.

Nevertheless, the UN human rights framework does provide rights and entitlements for individuals, mainly states in the human rights treaties (United Nations Human Rights Office of the High Commissioner 2016) as well as the Hundreds of regional human rights treaties, such as the one by the European Convention on Cyber Crimes (Convention on Cyber Crime 2001) or the UN Guiding Principles for Business and Human Rights (United Nations Human Rights Office of the High Commissioner 2011). These treaties all could be applied anywhere in the world in the light of protecting human rights such as the right to human security and privacy, that of freedom of participation and expression, of professional development or education based on gender equity, and access to information or development.

With this approach, the Internet is seen as a tool and a network that allows different digital devices to connect and communicate, but behind each service provided within this network, there are people and institutions that can be held accountable for the breach of data and violation of privacy or fundamental freedoms. The lack of justifiability and liability of actors and institutions that provide online service can be faced through global agreements among states but also with the measures already taken by users and private companies as illustrated through the user-centered "security-circle." The controversy is about the means and the litigability of human rights norms and standards, and thus, a global agreement on the procedures of cyber public policy is still to be seen. But de facto it does not need a treaty or otherwise governmental-centered agreement; it can be informally agreed upon among the different state and nonstate actors and agencies, users, and companies alike and put into practice. The key issue is whether the contracting parties can agree on joint and neutral monitoring and enforcement mechanism for effective implementation of the agreement or treaty.

Of course governments, international organizations, such as the UN, or regional organizations, such as the EU or the OAS, alone cannot safeguard these rights, let alone enforce or protect them. But with the involvement of, for example, local administrations and courts, that is to say "server-located" entities that adhere and enforce these standards and protect users' human rights as well as with the collaboration of companies, it might succeed.

Over the last years, cyber-citizens and users have become more conscious of posting information and data that might potentially be used against them in international or national lawsuits, as seen in recent court decisions in Europe (European Court of Human Rights and Council of Europe 2015). Case law is about to be established and shows that it is possible to monitor and regulate the attitudes and behaviors of users and to establish a rule of law for the cyberspace. A new social contract between users and the network providers is to be achieved based on the two main avenues to pursue for. These are (1) to establish a societal and legally binding "cyber constitution" and (2) to establish global enforcement and monitoring bodies, such as a global cyber-court, multistakeholder committees, or otherwise rotating, participatory, and transparent governance regimes. This cyber-public policy regime would allow for collaborative work with national/domestic and local institutions, i.e., administrative or constitutional courts, NGOs, International Organization, or public administrations, to implement and enforce rights and duties of people moving in cyberspace.

With a 30% annual birth rate, the "cyber-society" is one of the fastest growing and thus in the urge for common rules, regulations, and laws particular for social networks which are the most commonly used services in the Internet such as Orkut, Baharatstudent Renren, Facebook, or LinkedIn. Although international governmental organizations, such as the IGF, AU, EU, SOE, or the International Telecommunication Union (ITU), aimed to respond to these needs by holding social network providers, such as Facebook, accountable as well as their users when posting hate speech language, their state powers and enforcement mechanisms often end at state borders because their mandate to protect human rights is entirely based on state sovereignty and governments.

What is thus needed is a new definition of Internet or cyber sovereignty. Thus, sovereignty would be based on similar criteria to that of national or domestic sovereignty, namely, to control and executive effectively and independently common norms and standards in a given space (formally: territory). A combination of rotating governance bodies and through active participation of various stakeholders, such control (or: governance) can be effectively executed. Charges, penalties, or even imprisonment in case of misconduct and misuse of cyberspace need to be executed in a similar way as international courts, such as the ECJ, the International Court of Justice (ICJ), and the ICC already do.

Apart from a definition of what effective cyber governance means, it is still up to this community how they apply global human rights norms to concrete cases of privacy, security, health, free expression, movement, and enterprises and give guidance to the various numbers of different actors that are involved in the design of the cyberspace regime and how to possibly regulate it. If ever established, the cyberspace governing body will be one of multiple stakeholders and actors including national, international, as well as private actors, such as representatives of companies, social networks, NGOs, and individuals.

The big challenge thus for cyber governance is how to protect data, uphold freedoms and privacy, and thus enhance users' trust in the Internet? How to realize neutral Internet, free from making commerce a prerequisite for access? There is on the one side the institutional and agency legitimacy which concerns service providers, governments, or private companies, such as Microsoft, Google, or Renren. These stakeholders seek legitimacy through users' trust. The way in which service providers and users interact will thus determine the regulation system of the future. Their need for security and safety of their data is absolute priority. Transparency and accountability mechanisms regulate the norms. Norms, standards, and regulation mechanism together compose what later can be called a "cyber constitution" which may even lead to establishing a global cyber court that cannot only issue penalties and judgments that have personal consequences, such as detention. Similar to international tribunal procedures or as illustrated with the example of the cyber justice laboratory at the University of Montreal, these sentences can be executed anywhere in the world.

Internet users that are residents of countries in which the rule of law and human rights are not complied to, will less likely trust the Internet than users that live in countries in which human rights are implemented and enforced. A lot depends on the behavior of institutions and the local environment whether or not users trust online services. In other words, people who have negative experiences with offline institutions and companies that are corrupt and little trustworthy will also not trust online and global institutions. The fact that they have no physical positive experience with good governance and trustworthy institutions is transmitted to the online world and the cyberspace they move in. That said, these users do trust services offered by companies and e-commerce, for example, credit card companies that are based in countries in which the rule of law is adhered to, and they can be held accountable for wrongdoings—but only if these trustworthy institutions are also accessible for and responsive toward them. That is why many of the e-commerce companies today invest millions in data protection and security systems (Corbitt et al. 2003).

Thus by using services outside their country or the state they live in, Internet users legitimate online companies by repetitively using their services and enjoy positive and nonabuse responses by them, i.e., when they order consumer goods through online services abroad which actually deliver after people have prepaid, as is the case for Chinese consumer who, if possible, rather purchases certain goods online abroad than inland. Positive experience with norm compliance through external stakeholders which increases the trust in these financial or commercial online sectors.

Having stated that the desire for more and better regulation in cyberspace is correlated to the desire for good governance and human rights-based regulation in the offline world, we can look back to societies who had been fighting these battles for a long time and won them, for example, in Europe. According to Max Weber, what makes a political regime and its institutions legitimate is that it allows for widespread engagement among its citizens or members that in return reward the regime with a certain belief or faith of legitimacy, the "*Legitimitätsglaube*." Thus, representatives of the regime and members of society have to jointly agree on the common rules and standards and thus the regulation regime they want to be governed by. This is best achieved through a democratic system in which free participation and exchange by all groups of society is anticipated. According to Weber "the basis of every system of authority, and correspondingly of every kind of willingness to obey, is a belief, a belief by virtue of which persons exercising authority are lent prestige" (Weber 1964, p. 382). Weber frames legitimacy as an important explanatory category to understand societal behavior and regime stability. That can also be transferred to a cyber regime in which faith by users in a particular social order produces social regularities that are more stable than those that result from the pursuit of self-interest, commercial benefit, or from habitual rule-following. If these participatory conditions for legitimacy are not met, regimes exercise power unjustifiably, and the commands they might produce do not entail any obligation to obey.

Thus, the more trust and faith in service providers users have because they can directly interact with them, that is, in complaints procedures, the more legitimacy they enjoy. In economic terms, this would also mean more benefit on a long-term basis and more stability of the regime. But in return it means that cyber regulations mean the willingness of stakeholders, may they be of political or commercial nature, to share power among them and allowing for actors to participate in the regulation regime that thus far had been excluded from any decision-making process, for example, minors, refugees or members of illiterate minority groups, etc. One of the challenges for participation arises from the large percentage of Internet users that are below 18 years old, an estimate of 30%.[2] By common offline legal standards, this group, approximately 600 million people, is not fully accountable nor of age to be a full participant in the decision-making of the cyber regime. But yet, these are active cyber citizens that even at an age of 14 already have the capacity to do full e-commerce or at the same time program bots and algorithms that can lame a whole water supply plant, because Internet technology allows them to do so. Thus, the cyber regime does not only urge us to shift and redistribute responsibilities but also to think about the age of those holding full responsibilities.

References

Corbitt, B. J., Thanasankit, T., & Yi, H. (2003). Trust and e-commerce: A study of consumer perceptions. *Electronic Commerce Research and Applications, 2*(3), 203–215. Accessed April 19, 2017, from http://www.sciencedirect.com/science/article/pii/S1567422303000243.

[2]Survey in the United Kingdom in 2016 illustrates the rate of Internet users below 18 years: Think Digital First (2016). Social Media Demographics. http://www.thinkdigitalfirst.com/2016/01/04/the-demographics-of-social-media-users-in-2016/. Accessed 19 April 2017.

Council of Europe. (2001). *Convention on cybercrime*. http://www.europarl.europa.eu/meetdocs/2014_2019/documents/libe/dv/7_conv_budapest_/7_conv_budapest_en.pdf

European Court of Human Rights and Council of Europe. (2015). *Internet: Case- law of the European Court of Human Rights*. Accessed April 19, 2017, from http://www.echr.coe.int/Documents/Research_report_internet_ENG.pdf

Identity Force. (2017). *Identity Force*. https://www.identityforce.com/blog/2016-data-breaches

Internet Governance Forum. (2016). *The internet governance forum*. Accessed April 19, 2017, from http://www.intgovforum.org/

Internet Society. (2016). *Global internet report 2016: Mobile evolution and development of the internet*. Accessed April 19, 2017, from http://www.internetsociety.org/globalinternetreport/2015/assets/download/IS_web.pdf

Mihr, A. (2016). Cyber justice: Cyber-governance through human rights and a rule of law in the internet. *US-China Law Review, 13*(4), 314–336.

Think Digital First. (2016). *Social media demographics*. Accessed April 19, 2017, from http://www.thinkdigitalfirst.com/2016/01/04/the-demographics-of-social-media-users-in-2016/

United Nations Human Rights Office of the High Commissioner. (2011). *Guiding principles on business and human rights*. Accessed April 21, 2017, from http://www.ohchr.org/Documents/Publications/GuidingPrinciplesBusinessHR_EN.pdf

United Nations Human Rights Office of the High Commissioner. (2016). *The core international human rights instruments and their monitoring bodies*. Accessed April 19, 2017, from http://www.ohchr.org/EN/ProfessionalInterest/Pages/CoreInstruments.aspx

Weber, M. (1964). *The theory of social and economic organization*. New York: Free Press.

Chapter 10
Cyber Governance

Cyber Governance is a public policy process and the way in which different actors interact and participate according to specific norms, rules, and regulations they impose upon themselves. Internet governance, as it is also called, refers to these procedures and how they impact the way the Internet is managed (Mihr 2014). In 2016, the International Working Group in Internet Governance, a UN and CSOs supported group, published its 10-year anniversary report and presented first findings and recommendations on Internet governance. It indicated, overall, the rapid and challenging development of "cyber-citizens" and the growth of access to the Internet in the Global South. The Internet has spread and by now is a truly global technology. The new and often young users bring new perspectives, norms, and cultures to governance and the involvement of these actors. However, despite these developments, the working group highlighted that in comparison to its first report in 2005, one element has remained the same, namely, that the Internet governance regime of the twenty-first century ought to be based on the multistakeholder approach; otherwise it will fail to govern the cyberspace at all (Drake 2016).

In response to this and the alarming news about the lack of trust and legitimacy that private companies suffer in their online business, the World Economic Forum, that is a leading governmental actor in promoting cyber economy and e-commerce, has thus launched during its 2015 annual conference a global agenda of digital or cyber governance. It includes the establishment of a set of formal (law) and informal (code of conduct) norms for state behavior, better legal mechanisms for addressing cross-border cybercrime, transparent national legislation for law enforcement, and endorsement of the need for encryption to protect the integrity of data. The agenda aims at fighting the breach of data but at the same time safeguarding (economic and trade) freedom in the Internet is pivotal for that important actor in the cyber governance regime (Bildt 2015). And during the 2016 IGF in Mexico, the various stakeholders, including governments, confirmed the transition of the stewardship of one of the most important governing organizations of the Internet, the International Assigned Numbers Authority (IANA), a worldwide association that monitors IP addresses and their networks and in

A. Mihr, *Cyber Justice*, SpringerBriefs in Political Science,
DOI 10.1007/978-3-319-60093-2_10

which governments and private organization from around the world are registered and in support. IANA contributes and replaces partly the Internet Corporation for Assigned Names and Numbers (ICANN) which acts for the private sector to provide technical assistance for resuming addresses on the Internet, such as *.com* and others. It is a nonprofit corporation created in 1998 to assume responsibility for IP addresses in the private sector, but it has resumed significant power in the multi-stakeholder world of the cyberspace as Milton Mueller (2002) has identified. ICANN controls the private space in cyberspace. There are hundreds of thousands of speculative and abuse registration under the *.com* domain which has infringed the level of trust in private actors in the cyberspace, too (Mueller, 2002). The involvement of IANA and other organizations in the IGF effort for better cyber governance is an approach to gain back trust in light of the breach of data including the abuses of IP addresses. At the core is the effort to make the private and commercial part of the multistakeholder community an equal part of the overall cyber governance regime. This is supported by the Internet Society Organization, although also criticized by other observers. But even though governments, companies, and CSOs have taken ownership of the term Internet or cyber governance over the past years, the initiative to establish such a governance regime came from the private sector. Co:llaboratory, for example, is a network of researchers and Internet activists that started to investigate possibilities of Internet governance a decade ago, initiated and financed by Google since 2010 (Co:llaboratory 2017). Other sponsors and partners followed but its main purpose is to maintain the efforts to allow the Internet to be a transparent and open tool for everyone focusing on commercial benefits. Internet governance and the multistakeholder approach were also born out of the needs of CSOs to protect free communication and assembly through the Internet without much involvement of governments. Even though that means that radical and anti-liberal forces, terror groups, and anti-democratic forces use the same tool to promote hate speech, images of rape, violence, and other atrocious images and messages—these violent acts on the Internet should be ruled out, but they should not be a reason for closing down the Internet as such. Thus, the striking remark in this context is the fact that multistakeholder-based cyber governance is not an invention by governments for the well-being of global commons of Internet users. Instead, it is an initiative of many private companies, CSOs, and pressure groups to avoid that governments gain back full and sole control over the cyberspace by regulating and controlling the access to it. Nevertheless, it is the public sector of each country that provides and allows for the infrastructure to access the Internet. In short, wherever governments or governmental organizations fail to provide good governance and safety for their people, the Internet provides the platform for private and commercial initiative to fill that infrastructural gap—but it will be without control and rules and these users sooner or later will withdraw from making use of the services. This can be observed in many Sub-Saharan countries in which the access to Internet has grown dramatically but the number of tools and providers used remains limited. People trust Facebook, YouTube, and WhatsApp as their means of communication, commerce, and interaction. But all of these companies are US based and not based on the African continent because they stand for some forms of accountability that is better than no accountability at all.

Because of these developments in the Global South, Stuart Brotman (2015), from the Center for Technology Innovation at Brookings, a US-based think thank argues strongly in favor of the multistakeholder governance approach. But he also raises concerns when keeping the different cultures and traditions among stakeholders in mind of which the majority does not enjoy the benefits of democratic environments; the engagement with and participation from different stakeholders with different profit and nonprofit orientated interests, the lack of legitimacy of some stakeholders, as well as the lack of inclusiveness and accountability in these countries as well as in cyberspace remain the main obstacles for a coherent Internet governance regime (Brotman 2015). But despite the factual problems and differences among stakeholders, it is a global democracy project of an unseen magnitude and dimension; regional efforts and "pilot projects" such as e-governance to learn to listen and to share powers and make compromises can build up a global cyber governance regime—are under way.

E-governance is part of the anticipated Internet governance regime. This method aims to allow for more participation by cyber citizens in the field of e-commerce and governmental decisions. But first, national authorities ought to guarantee the efficiency of e-governance by setting the legal and political frameworks and allow free and neutral Internet for all—regardless of their income or place of living. E-governance is part of public policy and a system to govern or manage public affairs online and through direct intervention, for example, with patients in the health sector or students in the education sector. Not surprisingly recent statistics have shown that countries with high levels of social capital and technical infrastructures (which is mostly the case in democratic countries) use e-governance more than countries with less infrastructures (United Nations 2012, 9 ff.). This is not only due to the higher technological development and infrastructure in these countries but also because Internet users in these countries trust the public online services more than they do in other parts of the world.

Yet another form of e-governance is e-democracy. It is using ICT to enhance existing democratic behavior and actions rather than creating it. It allows Internet users to use ICT to participate directly, quickly, and equally in the proposal and the larger decision-making process on the local, national, or international level. Countries like the Netherlands, Estonia, and Iceland have experience in it, even in public elections. The aim is to increase public and citizen participation via the Internet to quickly and directly reach common agreements, norms, rules, and laws to govern communities. The challenge remains whether quick and direct participation always allows for enough time to generate information, make up one's own thorough opinion, and the lack of direct human and physical interaction with other people and stakeholders might impair the decision and votes casted online.

E-governance and e-democracy ought to allow for free, equal, and neutral access for all. To participate in Internet-based elections or services, it needs to be easily accessible and allow for equal practice of political self-determination. And that is by far not the case for the majority of the world's countries. Therefore, it is shown that countries who score high on e-democracy also score high on democracy in general because of their technical and democratic offline infrastructure (Netchaeva 2002). Thus, there is a correlation between technical and democratic infrastructure that allows for a majority of citizens to use the Internet as one tool, among others, to participate in the public decision-making process, but only if it is free, equal, and easily accessible for every citizen of that specific country. That is what e-democracy is in a nutshell. Yet, there is no evidence and no causality that e-democracy leverages democratic behavior per se in countries that score generally low in democracy or are governed in an autocratic manner. Because e-democracy is only another way in which to build upon already existing good governance principles, such as accountability, responsiveness, transparency, and Internet citizen participation. There is no automatism or automatic causality between Internet access and democracy. In this line, Aim Sinpeng (2013) has investigated the level of state repression and censorship of the Internet in Thailand. He argues that the level of censorship does not depend on the level of consolidation of democracy in a country but on the cost-benefit analysis. Even democratic regimes such as the Thai one censor and use repressive tools to limit Internet access and use of their citizens, when the costs of repression are lower than their benefits. He calls the costs of repression "state coercive capacity online," the hegemonic ability of state authorities to control cyberspace by force (Sinpeng 2013). The costs are also defined by a weak civil society that cannot or will not protest against censorship or by a weak judiciary that is not entirely free to intervene in censorships. Interestingly enough, the quality of Internet governance within a particular country also correlates with the level and quality of democracy these regimes enjoy in the offline world (Democracy Barometer 2017). The online and offline correlation is closely connected. Modernization theorists argue that due to the fact that Internet access needs a good technical infrastructure, the likeliness for democratic development is higher in countries where people have access to cyberspace than in countries where this access is limited (Berman 2009). The fact that Internet-censorship has reached a level of daily annoyance and even penetrates domestic economies to flourish has led Reporters without Borders and Amnesty International to the launch the annual World Day against Cyber Censorship, March 12 of each year, to commemorate the thousands of bloggers and HRD who face prison because of their online activities.

The core question remains whether or not people can develop trust and confidence in these digital tools that allow them to be governed in a more democratic way? In order to draw a correlation, we can take a look at the general definition of democracy. It becomes evident that e-democracy technology, search engines, network providers, and social media can be used as tools or catalysts of opinions and behavior, but they do not automatically build up a democratic culture or country because democracy is one form of governance in which all citizens participate equally and freely to agree on common norms and standards, either directly or through representation, which lead to the creation of rules and laws under which they wish to be governed. If the core concept of democracy, namely, the "rule of the people" for the people, remains true (Greek: *demokratia*), then the multistakeholder approach has its appeal for good cyber governance. Therefore, it depends how the people in a society use the Internet or have access to it.

But with democracy and good governance going online, we face the similar challenges as with good or bad democracy offline. The difference is, as citizens of the cyberspace, we currently all face the same transition period from an (almost) anarchical space to one that is governed by rules and mechanisms. There seems to be only "bad governance" at the moment that needs to be turned into good governance of the Internet and the cyberspace. Thus, the steps and procedures for successful transition to democracy are the same in the offline world. In fact we observe similar process of transition and transformation of territorial offline governance regimes everywhere in the world. Quoting Samuel Huntington's observation of successful transitions to democracy, we see current parallels to past processes of democratizations (1992). In his 1992 written essay "How Countries Democratize," he concludes that if over a longer period extremist groups or private actors oppose the new democratic system or are deliberately excluded there will be no democracy, but if forces are in legal and thus democratic opposition, there will be a democratic shift. But more so, if democratic forces are in coalition, pacted or negotiated, with old "elites," then there will be a successful transition to democracy (Huntington 1992). That is to say, if the multistakeholder approach equally includes governmental, private, and civil actors in its decision-making procedures, Internet governance has a real chance to succeed. The IGF is the meeting and negotiating platform between old and new actors in the cyber governance regime. And if we look further into other classical definitions of successful establishment of democracy through transition, we find similar developments between the offline and the online world. Juan Linz, Alfred Stepan, Wolfgang Merkel, and Larry Diamond observed democratic regime change and the process of democratization. In their views a democratic regime is consolidated when it meets several interconnected and mutually reinforcing conditions. First, there has to be a free and lively civil society and second, a relatively autonomous and valued political society such as publicly elected representatives of government. Third, there must be a rule of law and independent judiciary and, thus, for example, a constitutional court or other supervising legislative and judicial bodies to ensure legal guarantees for citizens and human rights and, fourth, a bureaucracy that is useable and under the mandate by the new democratic government. Last but not least, there must be an institutionalized economic society as well as a vivid and free civil society (Linz and Stepan 1996, pp. 14–33). A cyber court that oversees the cyber constitution and governing bodies that represent all stakeholders of the Internet regime would be the translation from the offline democracy to an online one. A robust civil (Internet) society is among the most crucial elements among these reinforcing conditions; they vigilate, monitor, participate in the online world and are the key factors when building trust or not in service providers. Thus, for the cyber governance regime, the same criteria apply as for a governance regime of a territorial state. That means that legitimation of a democratic regime is thus complete, if the behavior and habituation go beyond the normative constitutional commitment to democracy and when all relevant actors regard democratic laws, procedures, and institutions as the "only game in town" (Diamond 1999, p. 65). Democratic (cyber) transition is complete when sufficient agreement has been reached about political procedures to produce an elected government, when this government de facto has the authority to generate new policies and when the executive, legislative, and judicial power generated by the new democracy does not have to share power with other nonelected private or radical groups (Linz and Stepan 1996). Consequently, the challenge for the IGF is to develop criteria under which to select all relevant actors and stakeholders to participate in the constitutional assembly and make them agree on common rules and standards. In a second phase, the have to develop independent and neutral governing bodies and mechanisms that monitor control, implement, and enforce these rules. But the main challenge remains the criteria under which to select the stakeholder in the multistakeholder decision making process. Thus, the questions that may arise are: Who are these stakeholders and who is eligible to participate, who is representing what sector, interest group or user community, and is there a geopolitical balance, North and South, and equal access for everyone? Or more so, who will be excluded and not participate in the stakeholders governing bodies? Again, human rights and good governance criteria might be one benchmark by which to assess these stakeholders and another the stakeholder's record of human rights compliance and to what extent this actor or company and institution has done harm to others in the cyberspace?

An informal cyber social contract, a first agreement on norms, standards, and mechanism, is the basis for setting up more complex criteria among which to choose who should later participate in the smaller circle of decision makers. All four billion Internet users and providers cannot equally participate but need to issue a system of delegation (similar to political parties) which adequately and proportionally represent them.

The UN's agenda 2030, in the frame of the SDGs, includes e-governance as a tool to reach the goals. The UN argues that the socioeconomic development and human rights compliance can only be reached by including as many of the marginalized groups as possible. One way of reaching out to them and include them is e-governance through Internet, for example, by informing them via social media about agricultural development tools, education, literacy and health programs, child protection, and women defense tools. The UNDP seeks it as a major tool in achieving the SDGs because e-governance can support the implementation process of human rights in all aspects of life: health, governance, environment, and so on. This new framework is led by 193 UN member states plus the participation from external stakeholders, such as civil society organizations, the private sector, and businesses as well as academia and scientists. Reaching out to these target groups through the Internet can ensure that public institutions are effective, responsive, accountable, and representative through e-government and other e-governance means. This also carries the risk that an international agency, such as UNDP, bypasses governmental policies by interacting directly with citizens in need in the respective country. There is and there will be protest by domestic governments when they sense that these "development policies" interfere with their own power domain, because e-governance includes fostering public sector capacities and public–private partnerships at national and subnational levels, strengthening regulatory framework for businesses, preventing corruption, and promoting the transparent and sustainable management of public goods and financial and natural resources (United Nations Human Rights Office of the High Commissioner and UNDP 2012).

International relations and regime theories support the constructivist approach to a new global cyber governance regime. The fact that norms shape state and nonstate actors' behavior is not new. Advocacy coalition models, as found in public policy formulation processes, use international human rights norms to pressure their domestic governments to implement and enforce them. Governments usually respond to this pressure in one way or the other, either by engaging and promoting human rights or through censorship of online activism. The battles about power on the domestic level are already fought in cyberspace, regardless of how small the country of concern is. Nevertheless, even the most suppressive countries and regimes cannot stop the influence and power human rights and good governance norms have on people and Internet users. To promote them, organizations and CSOs include an array of technologies, regulatory measures, laws, policies, and tactics for commercial, political, or private reasons beyond border control but based on norm diffusion (Deibert and Crete-Nishihata 2012, p. 349).

The UN as well as the EU and other intergovernmental organizations, such as the SCO, have therefore launched a number of declarations or binding agreements on how to use or combat misuse of data in cyberspace and yet allow citizens free and open access to information, which is among their basic human rights. Some of these agreements resulted in the protection, and others in the violation, of human rights. Over the years, there have been some UN Resolutions on "cyber security" that are worth taking a closer look at later. Although major players in this arena such as Russia, Iran, and China do not want legally binding treaties for which they are not in full control, they also support these developments. Nevertheless, social networks gain ground even in the most suppressive regime. The so-called new social movements are beyond legislations, because their "members" and Internet-based stakeholders are visible but not necessarily residents of that particular country and thus dare to show and express their claims and desires to change regime habits. Therefore, these networks and movements cannot be declared anti-democratic just because they act beyond state borders or statehood. Instead, they share global values, among which the human rights values and norms are the most common ones. The fact that many monitoring institutions set agendas, such as the Freedom house index on the "Freedom of Net" to assess whether a society enjoys freedom to information, association, or privacy, is not surprising. The LSE media platform established in 2011 deals with these issues, aiming to assess the relationship between media communication, networks, and individual stakeholders, and how they solve and govern challenges and problems (London School of Economics 2017).

These initiatives also indicate that social networks are horizontal in structure as opposed to governments and sovereign states, which act vertical and hierarchical. In any future cyber war scenario, there will be thus no end or peace agreement—as known from offline wars—because weapons, such as cyber viruses or war bots, are repetitive and follow their own endless dynamics. There is no peace contract because there are no real-life opponents who could contract it and thus, this part of the cyber regime also has to be dealt with differently in the future because territorial governance is no longer the natural boundary (Mihr 2014).

Nevertheless, the creation by some governments of "new virtual enemies" in persons, such as the WikiLeaks founder Julian Assange or the whistleblower Edward Snowden, illustrate that cyber governance regimes cannot be without personalizing stakeholders and holding them accountable—whether this is justified or not. Persons, such as Julian Assange, Chelsea Manning, and Edward Snowden, not algorithms have become the faces that made the shortcomings of governmental control Internet security visible. Governments often label whistleblowers as security threats, even so they only illustrate and use the gaps, leaks of deficits of the currently cybersecurity regime. They are proxies that resemble that governments fear to lose control over cyberspace—which they alone never controlled in the first place. How to close these governance gaps will be part of the governance regime for the cyberspace.

References

Berman, S. (2009). *What to read on modernization theory*. Accessed April 19, 2017, from https://www.foreignaffairs.com/articles/2009-03-12/what-read-modernization-theory

Bildt, C. (2015). *What is the future of cyber governance?*. Accessed April 19, 2017, from https://www.weforum.org/agenda/2015/10/what-is-the-future-of-cyber-governance/

Brotman, S. N. (2015). *Multistakeholder internet governance: A pathway completed, the road ahead*. Accessed April 19, 2017, from https://www.brookings.edu/wp-content/uploads/2016/06/multistakeholder-1.pdf

Co:llaboratory. (2017). Accessed April 19, 2017, from http://www.collaboratory.de/w/Partner

Deibert, R. J., & Crete-Nishihata, M. (2012). Global governance and the spread of cyberspace controls. *Global Governance, 18*(3.) Accessed April 19, 2017, from https://www.questia.com/library/journal/1G1-301181778/global-governance-and-the-spread-of-cyberspace-controls.

Democracy Barometer. (2017). *Ranking*. Accessed April 19, 2017, from http://www.democracybarometer.org/ranking_en.html

Diamond, L. J. (1999). *Developing democracy: Toward consolidation*. Baltimore, MD: Johns Hopkins University Press.

Drake, W. J. (Ed.). (2016). *The working group on internet governance – 10th anniversary reflections*. Association for Progressive Communications.

Huntington, S. P. (1992). How countries democratize. *Political Science Quarterly, 106*(4), 579–616. Accessed April 19, 2017, from https://www.jstor.org/stable/2151795?seq=1#page_scan_tab_contents.

Linz, J. J., & Stepan, A. (1996). *Problems of democratic transition and consolidation: Southern Europe, south America, and post-communist Europe*. Baltimore, MD: Johns Hopkins University Press.

London School of Economics. (2017). *Media policy project*. Accessed April 19, 2017, from http://blogs.lse.ac.uk/mediapolicyproject/programme/

Mihr, A. (2014). *Good cyber governance, the human rights and multi-stakeholder approach*. Accessed April 19, 2017, from http://journal.georgetown.edu/category/symposia/cyberissues/

Mueller, M. L. (2002). *Rule the root, internet governance the taming of cyberspace*. Cambridge, MA: MIT Press.

Netchaeva, I. (2002). E-government and e-democracy. A comparison of opportunities in the north and south. *The International Journal for Communication Studies, 64*(5), 467–477. Accessed April 19, 2017, from http://rcirib.ir/articles/pdfs/cd1%5CIngenta_Sage_Articles_on_194_225_11_89/Ingenta914.pdf.

Sinpeng, A. (2013). State repression in cyberspace: The case of Thailand. *Asian Politics & Policy, 5*(3), 421–440. Accessed April 19, 2017, from http://onlinelibrary.wiley.com/doi/10.1111/aspp.12036/abstract.

United Nations. (2012). *E-Government Survey 2012. E-Government for the people*. New York: United Nations.

United Nations Human Rights Office of the High Commissioner, & UNDP. (2012). *Global consultation on governance and the post-2015 framework: Concept note*. Accessed April 19, 2017, from http://www.worldwewant2015.org/node/277876

Chapter 11
Social Cyber Contract

Sir Tim Berners-Lee, who co-designed the World Wide Web in the late 1980s, was one of the first pioneers to call for a Magna Carta for the web. In the view from the early days on the web has come under increasing attack from governments and corporate influence and that new rules are needed to protect the open and neutral system that does not only uphold human rights but also protects them (Kiss 2014). This demand for a cyber constitution, Magna Cyber Chartas, and social contracts for the Internet is thus as old as the creation of the Internet in the 1970s (Madison 2010). As illustrated earlier in this book, research on cyber and Internet governance started in the 1990s, and until today it follows the logic that if there is a new "cyber territory" in sight, people who settle in it need to design a governance regime. However, before doing so, one has to know what kind or territory it is, how its natural borders are, what the climate, and where the fertile grounds are. And establishing a new governance regime needs morally and politically as well as legally agreements of all settlers—a social contract.

Thomas Hobbes, John Locke, and Jean-Jacques Rousseau are known proponents of a moral and political social contract theory that lasts until modern times. Rosseau anticipated with his Social Contract from 1762 to "show how we can live in the chains of society without compromising our freedom" (Rosseau 1762, p. ix). He highlights the role of civil society, of citizens, which promises a free and equal relationship between the individual and the state. John Rawls' theory of justice follows that line of thought by highlighting the role of all actors in a society, not only governmental or private ones. The current efforts social contract for cyber governance is not written yet, but to the dotted line, it contains rules and principles that have shaped the Internet's development including rough consensus decision-making. Key to such a contract is the idea that private investments and interests (cyber economy) are guaranteed, but always in balance with the added greater idea of social justice, economic growth, protecting resources and commons (data), and well-being of all. User's rights ought to be protected by the requirement to provide service at government regulated rates. This idea is similar to the 2016 claims by leading politicians for a Digital Fundamental Rights Charter in the EU.

A. Mihr, *Cyber Justice*, SpringerBriefs in Political Science,
DOI 10.1007/978-3-319-60093-2_11

Any social contract includes elements of justice and how to best reach it. National and international courts can play a crucial role and are part of this cyber regime to safeguard such norms mentioned above and the case law already established. For example in 2010, the Supreme Court of Costa Rica ruled in one case that access to ICT becomes a basic tool to facilitate the exercise of fundamental rights and democratic participation (E-democracy) and citizen control, education, freedom of thought and expression, access to information and public services online, the right to communicate with government electronically and administrative transparency, among others. This includes the fundamental right of access to these technologies, in particular, the right of access to the Internet or World Wide Web (Res. N° 2010012790, Considerando V. 30.07.10). Mikkel Flyverbom calls this process "governing through visibilities" as being the first steps to a new governance regime (Flyverbom 2016).

More transparency reports will respond to the increased focus and demand by users for knowing how their data is aggregated, converted, or filtered and whether public data and information is trustworthy or not, i.e., through data profiling of people. But transparency alone does not provide insight into the agreement or relationships between states and service providers. Thus, Flyverbom (2016) goes on and argues that Internet platforms, such as Google, Twitter, and Facebook, provide a link between humans and technologies because they are constructed by software engineers. They are complex organizations full of people and engaged in strategic attempts to shape political agendas and cultural formations (Flyverbom 2016). This is one reason why they are part of the multistakeholder approach. But in line with Jeffrey Sachs, he also argues that the big data, what he calls the "data doubles" generated in cyberspace can visualize knowledge and produce more accurate truth about what people are really concerned about. Thus, Internet governance in his eyes is about the management of visibilities (data) and their relation to the processes of ordering (Flyverbom 2016). Nevertheless, what Flyverbom's assessment lacks is to address the way and means of holding the stakeholders accountable in this new order regime.

Similar to the concept of corporate social responsibility (CSR) or private public partnerships (PPP), in which private companies often in collaboration with the public sector have to ensure that human rights are guaranteed and standards upheld among their employees, in their products, in their marketing concepts, and for their customers—the concept of human rights in cyberspace. Everyone who uses the Internet and makes use of cyberspace has the responsibility to protect and respect private data and freedom of information. The Internet users, providers, companies, or governments alike can be made responsible for violating rights and also for protecting them. That is to say, individuals, companies, or governmental authorities who violate one's privacy can be held accountable through institutions, such as authorities and courts, in the countries or unions (AU, EU, OAS, etc.) they are resident of. Any international or global agreement that manifests human rights in cyberspace ought to be co-signed by all stakeholders such as social networks and governments alike, further encouraging their compliance to it. Such an agreement only makes sense if every country government becomes party to it. So far, governments and national institutions are still the strongest enforcement mechanisms to guarantee the rights of their citizens and enforce them if needed—although they are no longer the sole one because companies, too, are increasingly held accountable for their human rights performance.

Jeremy Rifkin (2014), one of the proclaimers of the Internet being the Third Industrial Revolution, argues that the zero cost e-commerce that emerged in the 1990s through the Internet has led to a zero marginal cost society. It has taken the human race from an economy of scarcity to an economy of sustainable abundance because of the equal and almost unlimited possibilities the cyberspace provides for everyone. He argues that each communication matrix and innovation in history (book print, telephone, etc.) also transforms human consciousness by extending the empathic drive across wider temporal and partial domains, bringing human beings together in larger metaphoric families and more interdependent societies (Rifkin 2014, p. 298). But the downside of e-commerce in an ungoverned cyberspace has been that people in less wealthy regions of the world have no neutral access to the Internet and depend often entirely on the services provided by commercial companies that often breach their data because there is no protection.

A cyber social contract is one answer to the unresolved quest for more accountability, trust, and legitimacy of e-commerce actors. Such a contract addresses not only the values, norms, and morals of a society but also the legitimacy and credibility of the institutions of the state—in our case the Internet as a network of state and non-state actors in relation to the individual users. Social contract arguments typically posit that users or cyber citizens have consented to surrender some of their freedoms and submit to the authority of the service provider, for example, by agreeing on the business terms marked in the bottom line of the providers' service page. In exchange for the free online services, such as in social networks and online-shopping portal, we give off our private data or bytes. The question of the relation between these fundamental freedom and privacy rights, that mark everyone's dignity and human security, therefore, is a core aspect of social contract theory for cyberspace.

Nevertheless, our understanding of legitimacy concepts still comes from our experience with the offline world. Our governance concepts are based on the experience of territorial state institutions and physical borders. We simply do not know yet how cyber governance will be fundamentally different from governing a country or a province. Some of these aspects have come up during the court cases at the European courts over the past years—such as the question: Who can be held responsible and how? Sovereignty is still state-based and connected to jurisdiction over a specific territory, i.e., when exercising international human rights law. Sovereignty in cyberspace is still difficult to determine and to justify. If legitimacy of any institution, company, or organization is achieved through the level of civic engagement or interaction in setting up, agreeing on common rules and standards is fundamental—but has not happened yet. Whoever is going to govern a new sovereign cyberspace needs to foster a high level of engagement and interaction as well as responsiveness in order to enjoy legitimacy and trust (Weinberg 2012).

Constructivists explain why some argue that norm and human rights diffusion impacts the way national jurisdiction (also in the case of cybercrimes) applies and changes the way we think about state borders and nation state as such and how we interact on different levels (Heintschel von Heinegg 2012). One element of enjoying high level of legitimacy is if there is a functioning judiciary. Transparent and independent jurisdiction can serve as a lawful power to make or enforce rules and win trust. It is the foundation of cyber justice and implies that everyone has the duty to protect human rights in cyberspace as derived from the principle of territorial sovereignty. The International Court of Justice (ICJ) has, for example, argued that territorial sovereignty also implies obligations to protect human rights in cyberspace and of that sovereignty gets violated by technical companies or servers that are based within one's own territory; the state is responsible—regardless whether online or offline. Because even cyberspace requires the existence of some physical architectures, somewhere (Heintschel von Heinegg 2012, 2013). In response to this debate on whether the Internet can weaken or strengthen sovereignty and legitimacy of state institutions, UN Special Rapporteur de La Rue recommended states to review national laws regulating online surveillance and update and strengthen laws and legal standards that can hold actors accountable even if they do not reside in one's own country. Communications surveillance should be regarded as a highly intrusive act that potentially interferes with the rights to freedom of expression and privacy and threatens the foundations of a democratic society. Thus, La Rue argues that legislation must stipulate that state surveillance of communications must only occur under the most exceptional circumstances and exclusively under the supervision of an independent judicial authority (La Rue 2013, para 81).

References

Flyverbom, M. (2016). Disclosing and concealing: Internet governance, information control and the management of visibility, in Internet Policy Review. *Journal on Internet Regulation, 5*(3), 1–15.

Heintschel von Heinegg, W. (2012). *Legal implications of territorial sovereignty in cyberspace*. Accessed April 19, 2017, from https://ccdcoe.org/publications/2012proceedings/1_1_von_Heinegg_LegalImplicationsOfTerritorialSovereigntyInCyberspace.pdf

Heintschel von Heinegg, W. (2013). Territorial sovereignty and neutrality in cyberspace. *International Law Studies, 89*, 123–156. Accessed April 19, 2017, from http://www.usnwc.edu/getattachment/ff9537ce-94d6-49a8-a9ef-51e335126c1e/von-Heinegg.aspx.

Kiss, J. (2014). *An online Magna Carta: Berners-Lee calls for bill of rights for web*. Accessed April 19, 2017, from https://www.theguardian.com/technology/2014/mar/12/online-magna-carta-berners-lee-web

La Rue, F. (2013, April 17). *Report of the special rapporteur on the promotion and protection of the right to freedom of opinion, and expression, Frank La Rue: UN Doc. A/HRC/17/27*.

Madison, M. (2010). *Exploring legitimacy in internet institutions*. Accessed April 19, 2017, from http://jotwell.com/exploring-legitimacy-in-internet-institutions/

Rifkin, J. (2014). *The zero marginal cost society: The internet of things, the collaborative commons, and the eclipse of capitalism*. Basingstoke, Hampshire: Palgrave Macmillian.

Rosseau, J. (1762). *The social contract, or the principles of political rights.* 1998: Wordsworth Classic of World Literature.
Supreme Court of Costa Rica. (2010, July 30). Res. N° 2010012790, Considerando V.
Weinberg, J. (2012). Non-state actors and global informal governance — The case of ICANN. In T. Christiansen & C. Neuhold (Eds.), *International handbook on informal governance*. Northampton, MA: Edward Elgar Publishing.

Chapter 12
Conclusion: Cyber Justice

Ultimately, the claim for cyber justice is based on a globally agreed social contract and a good governance-based cyber governance regime of which (today) four billion users generally agree upon and in which they have the possibility to interact freely and protected. This is an endeavor of a new magnitude because of the size of cyberspace, the number of "cyber citizens," and the speed and innovations IT provides. But it is not impossible as illustrated above, if these governance regimes remain to be based on the basic idea of universal human rights norms and principles which are no longer disputed among the majority of world's population. Which in return is the same one that accesses and uses the Internet for private, economic, social, or professional causes. Good governance principles based on concepts of democracy help to design a cyber governance regime that manages these common interest of users and providers in the Internet and provide the grounds for cyber justice.

Secondly, governments have to learn to share power with private and civil actors, and states have to give up sovereignty over the Internet and cyberspace in the future. Private companies have to become more transparent in what they do with the data of their customers and at the same time more liable and accountable towards them. The way in which this regime is formulated and negotiated will pave the road to cyber justice. Cyber justice will depend on the level of trust and legitimacy these governance regimes enjoy. Current case law and international criminal jurisdiction, trade, public customary, and international human rights law and decisions have already framed the new role of duty-bearers and right holders towards more individual responsibility in the cyber governance regime.

Furthermore, it is about combating abuse and misuse of data in cyberspace and, thus, cyber injustice. The concept of "public privacy" defines the challenges and obstacles of the current regime that governmental authorities face. Thus far, the primary responsibility to protect human rights and, thus, privacy rights in cyberspace is still within governmental and state framework. Others, such as telecommunication companies like Vodafone or Telekom and search engines like Google or Bing slowly become more co-responsible with the Internet governance regime,

A. Mihr, *Cyber Justice*, SpringerBriefs in Political Science,
DOI 10.1007/978-3-319-60093-2_12

for the way they process and protect personal and business data, and for the way they make their algorithms transparent. Yet, parallel to this, the claims for multiple or shared responsibilities among companies, private users, CSOs, and governments are no longer to ignore and are grounded in the idea of a multistakeholder approach. Shared responsibilities among the different stakeholders to be held accountable for human rights compliance and other norm compliance in a borderless world are one way to manifest the multistakeholder governance regime (SHARES Research Project on Shared Responsibility in International Law 2017).

While there is no lack of human rights standards or law in the offline and online world—and no need for any additional digital rights charter—the deficits of compliance and respect lay in the insufficient, corrupt, and weak measures and mechanisms that would allow us to comply and adhere to these standards. Most of them are only national and not global, let alone cyber. Therefore, the global cyber regime has to develop innovative ways and global mechanisms to monitor and enforce global human rights standards that go beyond existing national measures—a global cyber court is one way to fill this gap.

The existing common global norms and laws ought to be framed for the needs and purpose of Internet users by a multistakeholder community, regional organizations, and Internet users. This might more likely guarantee the inclusion of the "public" (the Internet users) and the protection of our privacy, namely, our civic and social human rights in the context of health, family, work, information, business, communication, etc. The quest for cyber justice is a logical consequence of this of which ICT is a key tool. To conduct, for example, trials online via the Internet can speed and strengthen up justice processes and procedures, but testimonials have to be trustworthy and personal data has to be safe and secure (Kastner 2013; UDEM Nouvelles 2013). Nevertheless, if it is technically possible, it might be one innovative way to attain justice and protection of human rights in cyberspace for users in all parts of the world.

In that, the UN Resolution from December 2013 phrases the quest for a cyber justice regime based on commonly adhered standards, rules, and regulatory procedures—namely, that member states emphasize that illegal surveillance of communications, their interception, and the illegal collection of personal data constitute a highly intrusive act that can violate the right to privacy and freedom of expression and may threaten the foundations of a democratic and peaceful society (UN General Assembly 1 November 2013). In order to combat the threats that exist online, they have to collaborate, exchange data, and share power, which eventually also leads to sharing power and sovereignty. With this resolution, UN member states recall their own obligation to ensure that measures taken to counter terrorism or other security threats comply with international human rights norms and do not violate it. Therefore, the 2013 resolution calls upon states to take measures to put an end to violations of those rights and specifically to establish independent oversight mechanisms of cyber governance capable of ensuring transparency and accountability of state surveillance of communications, their interception, and collection of personal data. It is the urge for a new rule of law in cyberspace and, thus, a new notion of cyber justice.

References

Kastner, P. (2013). *Cyberjustice in the context of transitional justice.*. Accessed January 1, 2017, from http://www.cyberjustice.ca/en/publications/cyberjustice-in-the-context-of-transitional-justice/.

SHARES Research Project on Shared Responsibility in International Law. (2017). Accessed January 1, 2017, from http://www.sharesproject.nl/

UDEM Nouvelles. (2013). *World Bank draws on expertise of Université de Montréal's cyberjustice laboratory*. Accessed January 1, 2017, from http://nouvelles.umontreal.ca/en/article/2013/02/11/world-bank-draws-on-expertise-of-universite-de-montreals-cyberjustice-laboratory/

UN General Assembly. (2013, November 1). *The right to privacy in the digital age*.

The manufacturer's authorised representative in the EU is Springer Nature Customer Service Centre GmbH, Europaplatz 3, 69115 Heidelberg, Germany. If you have any concerns regarding our products, please contact ProductSafety@springernature.com

Printed and bound by CPI Group (UK) Ltd, Croydon, CR0 4YY
25/09/2026
02222857-0016